Jo Brand started life as a good little girl, became a bad one for quite a bit, but now she's gunning for Reformed 'Man Hunter' turned National Disgrace.

Being grumpy has enabled her to react in a perfectly reasonable way to things that, in the past, she might have suppressed for the sake of keeping the peace/being polite/not making someone angry, Added to which, starting comedy at thirty (and as an ex-psychiatric nurse) meant she gave much less of a toss about what other people thought of her.

The host of several TV shows including Channel 4's award-winning *Through the Cakehole*, Jo has made legendary appearances on many others from *Have I Got News for You* to *Would I Lie to You?* to *QI*.

She is married, has two daughters and lives in London.

Praise for Born Lippy

'A hilarious must-have bible for anyone wanting to get gobby ... So smart, so funny. I wish I'd had it years ago' Sarah Millican

'A must-read guide to life as a woman' Helena Kennedy, *Mail on Sunda*

'The humo[...] [...]day Tim[...]'

'Moving, funny and most of all useful' *Scotsman*

'Funny, feisty and full of life ... I loved this book' Paul Schofield, *Good Morning*

'Sassy ... feisty and funny' *Sunday Express*

'Funny, clever and rude. Just like Jo' Morwenna Banks

'Engaging and witty, just like her comedy ... Informed and insightful' *Culture Calling*

'If you want to get really useful advice about life's problems, go to someone who has messed things up, admitted it, then got back on track. Jo Brand is such a person' *Daily Mail Weekend*

Born Lippy

How to Do Female

JO BRAND

JOHN MURRAY

First published in Great Britain in 2018 by John Murray (Publishers)
An Hachette UK company

This paperback edition published in 2019

1

A CIP catalogue record for this title is available from the British Library

Paperback ISBN 978-1-473-68773-8
eBook ISBN 978-1-473-68774-5

Typeset in Sabon LT by Hewer Text UK Ltd, Edinburgh
Printed and bound in Great Britain by Clays Ltd, Elcograf S.p.A.

John Murray policy is to use papers that are natural, renewable
and recyclable products and made from wood grown in sustainable
forests. The logging and manufacturing processes are expected to
conform to the environmental regulations of the country of origin.

John Murray (Publishers)
Carmelite House
50 Victoria Embankment
London EC4Y 0DZ

www.johnmurray.co.uk

For Griffo

To my funny, generous, kind, enthusiastic, tireless,
talented, creative, idiosyncratic, sensitive, radical,
adventurous, socialist, feminist friend.

We had so many pelvic-floor-threatening laughs.

We all miss you loads.

CONTENTS

No men have been harmed in the writing of this book.

Introduction

BEING LIPPY

When I was about five, something happened that amused my family enormously. We lived on the kind of modern estate that wouldn't have been out of place in an English remake of *The Stepford Wives*. I was in the front garden when a friend of my mum and dad's walked past. It was summer, very hot and I was wearing a summer dress. As this family friend passed, he stopped to say hello and said, 'You look very pretty,' to which I replied, 'I know.' He burst out laughing and moved on.

Obviously, the manners and humility my parents drummed into me throughout my childhood had taken a day off. I was, for a few seconds, the Kentish child version of a fifteen-year-old YouTuber: temporarily in possession of supreme in-your-face confidence without a glimmer of self-doubt. He told everyone in my family and they all had a good laugh. After that it was brought up every so often, as a jokey example of an out-of-character, weird way for a girl to behave.

That was before the values of cynicism, misogyny and societal expectations sent me off in a different direction . . .

The fact of the matter is that I was just being honest, as is every child at that age, before we (and I know more about the female in this instance) are battered (some of us literally) into submission by the complex network set up by a secret, powerful and all-encompassing global conspiracy to keep women in their place.

Feminist sensibilities were in their infancy when I was born and in my lifetime I have seen enormous changes. I started as a good girl, became a bad one for quite a bit and have been accused a few times recently of being a national treasure, mainly I think as an indirect way of saying I'm old.

As a good girl, I was obedient, helpful and hard-working at school. I never talked back to my mum or dad and did my homework and chores. I looked neat and my hair was always brushed. This idyllic period of my life started to melt away with the onset of adolescence and a complicated fusion of hormones and horrible family dynamics. My dad had always suffered from depression and his behaviour and mental health both deteriorated as I approached the age of fourteen-ish. Home became a battlefield and I ended up walking out at sixteen, having had to choose between the boyfriend they hated and my hated family life. I couldn't wait to get out.

The very act of giving advice does imply that one thinks one's advice is worth hearing and that sounds mighty arrogant, doesn't it? Although advice is traditionally transferred verbally from the world-weary old boot to the fresh-faced, naïve young thing about to depart on the inevitable bloody 'journey' through life, it's undeniable that some people are just very fond of the sound of their own voice, whether they know what they're talking about or not.

I worry about writing a book in which I impart my 'wisdom' to my 'daughters', or in other words, 'females who are very much younger than I am and have some hope and optimism left'. Not least because it makes me sound like a raddled old misanthropist, which is, coincidentally, my Mumsnet user name. I'm not really a misanthropist, but I do have an annoying 'been there, done that' mentality on my bad days. Think of it more like my being a bit further along on the trip and bellowing back warnings at the younger optimists many stations behind, in the vain hope it will be useful, before I reach my destination and enter the great big goods yard in the sky.

I can also be quite bad-tempered though and I have often wondered whether my advice would be of any use, given that it is probably grudging, a bit negative and rather pessimistic. I think the massive bonus about being a grumpy woman is that it enables me to react (in a perfectly reasonable way) to things that in the past I would have just suppressed for the sake of keeping the peace/ being polite/not making someone angry, which is a very womanly approach to the art of social interaction. So, for example, in the past, if someone had leaned out of a van, shouting abuse, I would have gone bright red, slunk further away on the pavement and mentally beaten myself up about it as many women still do. Now I simply do not tolerate it. I have metamorphosed from Snow White (purely behaviourally, you understand) into the Wicked Queen over the period of about thirty-five years.

Also if someone tries to insult, take the piss or offer me less than polite service, I'm now far more ready to go to war. It takes time to learn this though; sometimes in the past I got halfway there only to fall at the final hurdle.

Here's an example. Once when I was a nurse (in my twenties) I tried to pull into a twenty-four-hour petrol station, only to find my way blocked by dustbins. I went to the kiosk and there was a guy, feet up on the counter, eating a sandwich.

I said, 'Please can I come in, I'm out of petrol.'

He fixed me with a hard stare. 'I'm having my dinner.'

'Well, I'm really sorry to interrupt your food' – apologising! – 'but you are a twenty-four-hour service and my gauge is on red.'

He looked at me again and said, 'I'm having my fucking dinner. Piss off.'

I pissed off, but I was pretty incensed by this time and totally uncharacteristically, rather than just putting up with it, I went home and phoned the head office and reported him.

The following morning there was a ring on my doorbell. A man in a suit introduced himself as from the company who owned the petrol station and asked me what the man looked like who had been rude to me, because he was on his way to sack him.

Oh, bloody hell, this had gone too far. I didn't want the guy sacked. So I told Mr Suit I couldn't remember what he looked like. Exasperated, he told me there were only two possibilities: tall and blond or short and dark. I continued my ridiculous pantomime of not being able to remember and eventually he got fed up and left. Like a coward I then avoided the garage for a few weeks, hoping I hadn't been responsible for someone losing their job.

I suspect there are many out there who wouldn't lose any sleep over this – but it indicated to me that when it ultimately came to the crunch, I would probably always back off.

Maybe that's why I love comedy. When I'm doing stand-up, I find it much easier to face up to the things in life that irritate or anger me, because I feel as if I'm almost a different person up there with permission to be a right grump.

So, gingerly dipping my toe into the uninviting water of advice-giving . . .

Let's start with the wisdom learned through experience: you do things, fuck them up royally and then tell everyone else so they don't do it.

Here's another example. From a safety point of view, hitch-hiking is a complete no-no. We all know that. We are warned time and time again, but somehow there is a method for making that information bypass our brains.

I know this and I knew this when I was a teenager, but I still did it. I can just imagine my poor mum, strapped to a chair (because it's the only way I'd ever persuade her to read this), having a fluttery heart, even after forty-five years, when she reads this. I didn't do it often and on the whole got away with it, until the day I accepted a lift from three Irish guys in a lorry on the outskirts of Hastings when I was about fifteen years old.

Alarm bells started ringing when one of them got out to let me in so that I was sandwiched between them on the bench seat. Although there was no inappropriate touching or anything like that, straight away I knew I'd done the wrong thing and the sense of my impending doom hung heavy in the smoky air. I knew I had to get out as soon as possible. Shouting, 'Oh look, here's my destination, yes, sorry, it was only half a mile, I'm very lazy!' didn't seem like a plausible option and, as various ideas spun through my head – herpes, pregnancy, armed with a gun – I'm afraid I tried perhaps the most stupid one: I told them I was about to enter a convent, in the most chatty and throwaway fashion I could muster.

There was definitely a change of atmosphere. I held my breath as they looked at each other uneasily and then the slightly older driver swerved slowly to the side of the road and stopped. The door was opened, out I jumped and off sped the lorry's occupants without a word. I stood by the road just thankful that some vestige of decency had liberated me to fight another day, but I can assure you that was the second-last time I hitch-hiked. Not the last time I got into scrapes, by any means, but that's for later.

So, you're thinking, there she is, giving advice to us about something that just isn't relevant any more; that's like my grandma telling me always to wear a vest or I'd get pneumonia. I agree the context is outdated because hardly anyone hitch-hikes any more in this country, but thinking about the potential stupidity of what you're doing is a good thing to do in any context.

For example, would you meet someone from an online dating site in the middle of nowhere without telling anyone where you're going? Of course not and it's versions of every sort of putting yourself in danger as a young woman that are important to consider, from getting pissed and getting into a car whose driver says it is a minicab to going off into the night with a guy you've met five minutes ago. I also think a lot of the time women are polite and don't want to hurt people's feelings, which is why they are persuaded to put themselves in danger. How many women in John Worboys's taxi were a bit suspicious about being offered a drink but accepted it for the sake of not offending him? These split-second decisions can be so much more important than you realise at the time.

Advice is one of those things that is very easy to give and very hard to take. Anyone who tried to tell me what not to do when I was younger (and lots of people did) would be amazed to see me writing this book now because I ignored almost everything I was told. But that was because so much of it was either sermonising or so coloured by the experiences of the person giving it as to be nearly useless. Take, for example, my mum telling me as a teenager, 'Don't forget, all men are bastards.' Not so much advice as a statement, one presumed from her dealings with the male of the species.

Well, I didn't forget the advice, but experience has taught me that while it was possibly true at the time for my mum, who was splitting up with my dad (aka

'Everyman'), it was slightly too general to be of any real benefit to me. It's very easy to speak in massive generalities that tend to shave off any subtlety. I should know – I was 'a man-hater' in the press for years. Then, praise the Lord!, I got married so I could just narrow down all that antipathy into hating my husband. In one fell swoop I lost 'lesbian man-hater' and just retained 'scruffy and stout' in the press.

As the mother of two daughters, I often think about the rebellious teenager I once was and what advice I might have followed. I have fucked up enough times in my life to feel confident I have no special wisdom to impart to anyone approaching adulthood. But who cares? I'm going to do it anyway.

In *Born Lippy* I want to gather together all the things I wish I'd known, all the things I've learned and all the things I hope for the future. A century after women got the vote (albeit women of property over the age of thirty) it's time to take stock of what exactly it means to be female today. And if there's one thing we women are entitled to, it's having a bloody good moan about things big and small, so here goes.

I would love it if women everywhere could lay aside their natural instinct to be polite while at the same time avoiding any accusations of man-hating, which is why I used to do this joke to make the men in the audience feel at ease:

'The best way to a man's heart is . . . through his hanky pocket with a breadknife.'

All right, it didn't work for all of them . . .

1

YOUR FAMILY AND
HOW TO SURVIVE IT

I took my husband to hospital yesterday to have seventeen stitches removed. That'll teach him to buy me a sewing kit for my birthday.

If anything illustrates the struggle of different generations to get on with each other, it is surely the family holiday. We were always all a bit stressed for different reasons: everyone out of their routine, kids not really wanting to be with their parents all day for a week and both parents at times on the point of a meltdown.

I remember one particular gem of a holiday in Cornwall when I must have been about ten. I had bought and hidden a couple of little presents for my brothers. They somehow found out and had ransacked the rented holiday place from top to bottom until they found and devoured the chocolate I was going to give them when I got home.

Thinking I was not in parental earshot, I let rip with, 'You fucking bastards!'

Unfortunately my dad was in an adjacent room, and burst in, furious. My brothers' original crime was forgotten and I took the rap for a bit of well-chosen, and, I felt, very apposite language. Typical.

It seems too obvious to say that you have absolutely no choice in the selection of your family, a group of people with whom (if you manage to avoid a massive falling-out) you will spend a lot of your life, whether you like it or not. And many, many people don't like it. So, whatever family you are born into, if you end up with a good, loving, well-balanced couple of parents and some decent siblings, then you are very, very lucky indeed. On the other hand, if your family is a mix of egotistical, selfie-on-repeat oddballs with an eye for an easy buck . . . bad luck, Stormi.

Many adults spend a fortune asking therapists to explore elements of their childhood with them and sort out the wrongnesses in their heads, so they can move on and start living their lives properly – as if up until that point they had been floundering around in some sort of poisonous fog, ruining everything and making stupid decisions about things like relationships and their future.

Anyone traumatised during their childhood will inevitably sustain some emotional damage, but it is how they deal with it that really makes the difference. My dad's depression affected all of our family. The same goes for families with, for example, an alcoholic or drug-using member and/or any number of emotional difficulties. For quite a few of my teenage years I was frightened of my dad and that's not a good way to live your life.

The Fallout from a Nuclear Family Can Be Toxic

We call the usual family unit 'a nuclear family' because now we live in the modern age where it's no longer the case that the mother needs to churn out as many children as possible to ensure the family farm keeps going. And we don't live near our relatives any more, many of us. But I think the name 'nuclear' is very appropriate for a different reason. Families can be very volatile and dangerous groups. How do your relatives know how to say things that get right under your skin? How can parents be so embarrassing? How can your little brother make you homicidal? I can't promise to get to the bottom of your family but here are some thoughts that I use as my own emotional Geiger counter.

Billy Bragg tried to make it sound more charming: 'They tuck you up, your mum and dad,' but Philip Larkin's original 'They fuck you up, your mum and dad,' has far more resonance for me. That is because no one knows how to be a good parent and many couples simply carry on the bad parenting set up by their own parents (in some cases the damage is doubled as both spouses each bring a set of problems to the marriage). Anyway you get the message. All right, there are books a-go-go, websites, parenting classes, TV shows even, but they tend to be subject- or problem-specific and therefore do not knit together into a seamless script of how your parenting days should be. Many people we admire in the public eye have had a shit childhood and are trying to compensate for it by being in the limelight. And just when the attitude towards mental health is changing and the stigma dribbling away, the government cuts mental health services to the bone, making it almost worse than not having any.

Depression, cruelty, apathy, racism, sadism, inability to be a good friend/partner, deceitfulness and many other qualities can be traced back to one's parents, and those early templates are almost impossible to shed; and even worse we may not be conscious of them, but we have to learn to live with them. Let's be positive here: yes, for many children their parents do fuck them up but these problems are sort-outable. There are so many brilliant charities we can seek out if we realise we do need help. I would urge anyone who feels they're struggling to do everything they can to lift themselves out of the mire. It is possible.

Position in the Family

How often have you met people and thought, Bet they're the youngest child, they're so spoiled? However, we don't tend to go the whole hog and say when we meet someone else, 'Wow, why are they waving a huge flag? They are obviously bending over backwards to be noticed, they must be the middle child,' or, 'Hmm, serious and measured, they must be the oldest child.' Position in the family is important, but something we have to deal with. I also think the gender balance in the family adds a little *je ne sais quoi*. I am the only girl in my family and was forced at gunpoint by my brothers to watch football as a seven-year-old. By gunpoint I mean relentless teasing and the odd smack when my mum wasn't watching.

I think everyone knows their family inside out and therefore they're very aware of what triggers meltdowns. For example if someone in your family has an alcohol problem, best not to water the roses with their hidden bottle of vodka. Sorry, that isn't meant to be flippant but we can all see build-ups coming like a tornado, from miles away.

I think, invariably, the answer is to walk away. Trying to reason with a family member who rehearses the same script over and over again with your own over-used script is only ever going to result in a predictable row. While I'm on the subject, walking away for good may be the only option if you feel you've been trapped in a web of the same arguments and fights for years.

One useful bit of advice I got from somewhere is a version of 'actions speak louder than words'. People may go blue in the face telling you they're going to change, but if they don't, it's time to bugger off and it's the length of time you're prepared to wait for change that counts.

In the olden days you tended to have your traditional mum 'n' dad 'n' two kids family with Grandma round the corner for babysitting and the like. And however happy they looked from the outside (it was all about presenting a front), you can be sure some unsavoury things were taking place behind the curtains or the legacy wouldn't have been quite so many disturbed individuals. This is still the case in so many families but at least we are slightly more open, schools are more vigilant and social services, although stressed, do actually exist.

Now families exist along a continuum from traditional to about as freaky as you could imagine, taking in single mothers, single fathers, same-sex parents, trans parents, men married to sexy robots (all right, not that one but it's coming and so will the men be), and it's not that that matters, it's how much they love their kids.

Why haven't I referred to happy families and their issues? Because happy families don't need sorting out – lucky bloody them.

The simultaneously tragic and joyful thing about families, when you are very young, is that as a child you have nothing else to compare them with and so we all have our own individual version of a family we assume is just like everyone else's.

When I was growing up we were quite a nature-orientated family with lots of pets – dogs, cats, fish, hamsters, rabbits, tortoises and doves. Fairly often we would rescue injured animals and look after them until they recovered or died. This included a lot of baby birds who had fallen out of nests and one day my dad brought home an injured hare who was nursed back to health and became like a pet. However, one day, Harold (yeah, I know, very imaginative) struck out for freedom and we kids stood in the garden on a spring day shouting and begging our mum to stop him as he headed towards a waist-high fence (adult not child).

My mum did something I have always been stunned by: she sprinted after him and as he soared over the fence so did she, catching his back legs in mid-air. It was the most extraordinary performance and we stood clapping and cheering in the garden as she walked back round the neighbour's side path. When you're seven you tend to think your parent is at least seventy, so to see her hurdle a fence like that opened my eyes to the fact that my mum was her own person and very fit to boot (fit in the old sense of the word).

Given that all little kids assume their family is the norm, Mum being pissed is normal, not having breakfast is normal, being beaten is normal, having crisps for tea every night is normal (wish this had been my family), living in squalor is normal. Sadly, all these things and many more deprivations are 'normal' for many children.

As a society I think we all hope someone else will deal with problem families – a combination of social workers, the police, teachers and the health service will go charging in and sort it. And nine times out of ten they do their best. But not if they don't know about it.

If you're worried about something in your own family or someone else's, if it feels wrong – Do Something! Feel Free to Poke Your Nose In. Rather the embarrassment of having made a mistake than the truly awful consequences that are all too common today. Our society is changing gradually but a lot of people are still reluctant to breach the sanctity of families, unless someone is blatantly committing a crime in their garden in front of us while we are holding our camera phone.

Most of us have instincts about these things and there are plenty of websites offering advice as to how to go about it. So I seem to have started by asking you to Be a Responsible Citizen and Care About Others.

Let's hope my children are not reading this and getting straight on to Childline.

But while we're on the subject, thank God organisations like Childline exist. They certainly didn't when I was growing up. Kids just had to put up with whatever was going on in the family, and the local community helped by indulging in a form of support known as Turning a Blind Eye.

So, let's accept that families are not always happy and they don't behave how you want them to behave. What are the best ways to survive your family?

One problem is that we do tend to expect too much of family members. We are shown images of families in films, on ads, in books and on TV programmes but the disconnect between those images and our rather less primary-coloured home life is huge. Why isn't our mum dancing in the kitchen wearing a flowery dress and a smile while simultaneously producing a culinary delight worthy of *MasterChef* (or MistressChef as I prefer to call it)? Why is our mum slumped in a chair in the corner instead, knackered, having ladled out fifty shades of grey on to a plate and expecting us to eat it?

Before I had children I must have had a pretty poor imagination because I hadn't factored in the sheer hard slog of it all, the sleeplessness, the frustration, the bad-temperedness, all balanced by the joy that the little bundle you've got is made by you.

Sadly, we know some people experience the first set of frustrations but these are not alleviated by the joy of the child they've produced and they are the ones who struggle.

If parenthood is not quite working out as you hoped, the answer to this – and this answer will do for many of life's disappointments – is . . .

LOWER YOUR EXPECTATIONS

Lowering your expectations will not improve the actual situation but it will ensure you are not quite so unhappy with what you've got.

Let's take family 'occasions' for example. Times we are supposed to enjoy (imagine a regimental sergeant major repeatedly shouting that one word in your ear through a megaphone) yet think of the desperation with which most of us 'look forward' to family events.

The Family Wedding, the Family Christmas, these and many more family events can be imbued with a gravity and importance they don't really deserve, and if only people chilled out a bit they would be so much more fun. Instead everyone HAS (underlined three times) to enjoy themselves, smile as if their lives depended on it and woe betide the family member who gets a bit too pissed or says something inappropriate to Aunty Dardy. Yes, I did have an Aunty Dardy and I have absolutely no idea which name that was originally derived from.

I'm sure the last thing you want from me is parenting tips and that's good because you're not going to get them. And anyway, my parenting has very much been affected by the fact that some people know who I am – and that means that when I was out with the kids when they were small I was always very conscious of people watching us and it used to make me feel anxious that they were looking for some flaw in my perfect parenting skills. Thankfully the children behaved impeccably most of the time and I'm very grateful to them for that.

I have leaned towards the more liberal. I don't mean I send them out to buy drugs and say, 'And get a wrap for yourselves,' but on the other hand I don't stop them watching ITV because it's got adverts. Yes, my parents really did do that. And I tended not to breastfeed in public – didn't want that on the front of the *Daily Mail*.

The other thing I have tried to do with my children is keep them out of the public eye. That well-known cliché 'There's no such thing as a free lunch' certainly applies if you are a so-called celebrity with children. I used to get excited when I was invited to Euro Disney or to go on a pirate ship ride down the Thames with the children until I realised that the price was all our photos in *OK!* magazine and me spouting some bollocks about our family habits. So we didn't go on any of them – sorry, girls.

So the upshot of all this is some minimal, possibly useless information about how to survive some of the most dangerous events of the family year.

Christmas

Avoiding conflict at Christmas is easy if you either convert to another religion or become a conscientious objector to Christianity. Changing your religion, however, doesn't rule out the whole issue of avoiding a family Christmas, it just means you will have get-togethers with your family at different times of the year.

So don't think it's going to be brilliant this year (again) when you know it's going to be mediocre verging on shit. If there is a tendency for rows to arise, spend a shorter time at whichever relative's house it is, or resolve not to rise to the bait of your dad's annual speech on immigration. Go out for a walk – that'll unite the family . . . We all hate a walk on Christmas Day, hardly anything open so you can't even buy any sweets even though you've just consumed fourteen thousand calories for lunch. Failing this, pretend to be asleep for as long as you can.

Family Holidays

Once you've lowered your expectations make sure you're going on a general kind of holiday that all members of the family like, not just an archaeology break near Hadrian's Wall. Give everyone in the family enough time to do their own thing, unless they're under the age of twelve in which case they have to do what you say and resent you or incorporate the experience into a stand-up routine.

Actually ask the family – all of them – what they'd like so everyone feels they've had a say. And if they're a baby show them a map of the world and see which area they throw some food at.

Car Journeys

At least on car journeys these days everyone can live in their own little world of pain, pausing only to enquire about the ETA at the destination. This leaves you free in the front while you berate your husband about whatever you feel like, then look properly at him and see he's got headphones on as well.

Politics

Never discuss politics at home, especially if you live with Nigel Farage.

2

WHAT NO ONE TELLS YOU ABOUT THE FEMALE BODY

I went swimming in the sea recently. I plaited my bikini line so it wouldn't catch on any rocks.

My first proper set on stage in a comedy club was not very ladylike. I was wearing a big, white T-shirt, I put a blood capsule in my mouth, walked to the microphone, coughed and what looked like blood spattered all over my T-shirt and then I said cheerily, 'Must give up smoking.' I closed my set with a joke about how women are encouraged to refer to periods euphemistically so as not to embarrass sensitive male listeners.

I gave two examples:

'I've got the painters and decorators in,'
or,
'Arsenal are playing at home,'
then . . .

'but I prefer to say, "I've got a vast amount of blood squirting out of my cunt, vicar."'

To say the audience were shocked is an understatement; however there were lots of laughs, mainly I suspect from the women in the audience who were fed up of being herded into the Delicate Sensibility pen. Women have been having periods since time began and we're fed up with being made to feel something is wrong with us or we are slightly scuzzy because of it.

The female body is the focus of so much anxiety, desire, metaphor, crime, envy, hatred, fantasy, pain, disappointment, mystery, shame and grooming – in both senses. I could go on for pages, but you get the idea.

The oldest surviving human statue is female. It was carved from a mammoth bone 35,000 years ago. The Venus of Hohle Fels has huge drooping bosoms and enormous childbearing hips, and several other similar figures have been found, all with the same proportions. Some were even covered in red dye, which archaeologists have suggested was to evoke menstrual blood and fertility. It's cheeringly obvious what was seen as attractive in Palaeolithic times: which makes a joke of all those celebrities out there desperately following the Paleo diet to achieve skinny perfection. Cro-Magnon Posh would have been shunned.

Since then and across a series of increasingly male-dominated and male-run societies, a different ideal of a woman's body has controlled women, but who was it who decided what exactly that ideal should be? Was it a Greek sculptor, a committee of matrons, or just some pervy bloke? Who knows who the culprit was, but, my God, did women take notice. (My mother believes that the fashion industry demands models are so emaciated because it is run by gay men whose ideal is to make clothes for fourteen-year-old boys; please address all complaints about this to her.)

Women's bodies have always been assessed separately from their minds and personalities, and not only their bodies, but their individual bits have been critiqued, too. Women were always seen as more acceptable partners if their body and face looked good. As someone who is not actually in that group, I had always hoped that things might change as we became more civilised, and as equality marched forward, even though it is taking squillions of years, women would become more relaxed about their bodies.

In my day, the female body was still pretty much covered up, apart from a few grubby clubs where men with goggly eyes went to leer at women taking their clothes off. In public, though, women wore swimsuits that looked like a flowery fridge-freezer with two pointy bits, and bras were similar, with the conical upper bits of Madonna fused with a student nurse's bandaging exam gone wrong. Skirts were demure, cardigans practical, dresses for girls were like tents, and for women like slightly gathered-in tents. All designed to hide the female shape, although waists were pulled in and if you didn't have a twenty-inch waist you were no one.

All this changed in the sixties, as skirt-length gradually climbed upwards from the knees and towards the rude bits. And with freedom and liberation came choices, and women could begin to show as much of their bodies as they wanted. As the sidebar of shame that is MailOnline demonstrates, it won't be very long before fashion leaders pop out to the BAFTAs with absolutely nothing on at all, given that at the moment we are being treated to side-boobs and under-boobs ... (oh God, how old are these people?)

However, if we go back in time, language has always been sexist, misogynistic and any other word you can think of for unfair etymological treatment of women. So 'hysteria' comes from the Greek word for womb and I'm sure you're all aware that if women lost their equilibrium in those days, it was assumed that this was because their womb was wandering unhelpfully around their body* and confusing them; 'vagina' is the Latin word for sword sheath† (ouch!); and the term for the general genital area, 'pudenda', literally means 'things to be ashamed of'.‡

Let's look at a few fascinating bits of the female physique that have had net curtains unnecessarily drawn around them, which incidentally reminds me of an incident some years ago. I was having a smear test and I had assumed

---

* But where – a dirty weekend in the left calf?
† And we've all had a couple of little penknives popped in our sheaths, haven't we, ladies?
‡ (Although mine's not in great shape): so that's now my husband's nickname.

the position in a room with somewhat inadequate curtains when the young female doctor who was about to do the biz realised she had forgotten a piece of kit and left. I reckon someone stopped her on the way and invited her to pen a short novel because her absence seemed like an age. At one point the very scrappy curtains were drawn back and a couple of workmen peered in . . .

'Oh, sorry to disturb you, luv.'

Yes, I was disturbed for quite a long time after that.

The Wonder Down Under

Vaginas are amazingly stretchy – well, babies come out of them. And that's a conjuring trick far stranger than anything covered by the Magic Circle. But the really surprising thing is the clitoris. Although anatomists have known since the 1800s that the visible bit is just the tip of the iceberg, it has remained a medical curiosity, unmapped by many a male explorer (five points if you spotted the 'man-can't-find-the-clitoris' joke). While the penis is described in exhaustive detail in anatomies and textbooks, as late as 1948 *Gray's Anatomy* chose not to label the clitoris at all. (Maybe Gray should have gone to Specsavers – ten points.)

Until the twelfth week of pregnancy the genital tracts of male and female embryos are exactly the same, then they develop into the penis and clitoris respectively. If there were a game of orgasmic top trumps (now that's an idea), the clitoris would win hands down. It contains eight thousand highly sensitive nerve endings, double the nerve endings in the entire glans of a penis. Seeing how much less surface area it has, that makes it fifty times more sensitive. Save that fascinating fact for the next time you're in the middle of a row about how to load the dishwasher and hit them with it.

Societies have thought up all kinds of ways to try to control women's behaviour through controlling their sexual organs. The most horrifying is Female Genital Mutilation (or FGM), which is the ritual cutting or removal of some or all of the external female genitalia. It is designed ultimately to reduce women's pleasure in sex and thus to stop them straying. (Because we are no more than sheep with clothes on.) Unsettlingly, it is usually initiated and carried out by the women in the family, who see it as a source of honour, and who fear that failing to have their daughters and granddaughters cut will expose the girls to social exclusion. Health effects can include recurrent infections, difficulty urinating and passing menstrual flow, chronic pain, the development of cysts, an inability to get pregnant, complications during childbirth and fatal bleeding. There are no known health benefits. The world is changing but not fast enough for the 200 million women living today in thirty countries who have undergone these procedures. Lives are still being ruined and we need to do everything we can to stop this happening: it shows how vitally important it is to be able to talk openly about the female body.

What makes me chuckle are the male folk tales told about *vagina dentata* (Latin for 'toothed vagina') in some cultures about women whose vaginas have teeth that can bite off a penis. These stories are told as cautionary tales to discourage men from sleeping around. They can also prey on male castration anxieties as well as the fear that they may be diminished by a woman. I think my elderly vagina probably needs dentures at this point.

Wouldn't it be great if women everywhere embraced the idea that their vagina could be such a powerful weapon, rather than something shameful that needed to be silenced or at the very least some extra storage when you're shoplifting in John Lewis.

Bloody Periods

In my childhood, we didn't know much about our bodies, and physical development stages were so cursorily covered – at school, one thirty-minute lesson; and by parents, nought minutes – that I genuinely believed I was going to have only one period and then it would all be finished for life. I was eleven. I talked to my mum about this and expressed relief that this horror wouldn't repeat itself and she was forced to correct this assumption, leaving me devastated, because they're horrible, so frowned upon and so hidden – and so painful.

Although we are not allowed to discuss or allude to anything approaching a period in public still, they seem to be surrounded by huge, taboo blankets and we shroud anything to do with women's menstrual cycle in euphemism.

In the past girls and women were prevented from doing lots of things because of their periods. Washing your hair was out and the thought of anyone going for a swim while blood was squirting out all over the place was beyond the pale. These days you can't get away from ads showing women doing all manner of terrifying sporty things, safe in the knowledge that a tampon or whatever will prevent an embarrassing leak as you're abseiling backwards down K2 with a zebra slung round your shoulders.

But there's the small matter of the tampon tax. Periods cost women an average of £18,450 over their lifetimes. Why are tampons luxuries? Because men don't have periods, that's why.

The discovery of PMT was a joy (or maybe a woman invented it to enable us to behave badly). It was a feeling of bubbling rage with me and, when a man shouted some abuse out of a van at me, enabled me to go and rip his windscreen wipers off. I actually enjoyed it and it was guilt-free vandalism, very different from the sort of thing you do when you're drunk. I somehow felt self-righteously justified.

The Baby-Growing Experience

Of course one way of avoiding period pain is to get pregnant and replace it with birth pain – like all the period pain for a year fashioned into one big pain. Bad move. Having a baby seems to be quite a varied experience and I think that the expectation of how it will be has a pretty big psychological effect on the woman concerned. For example, I know several women who were absolutely terrified of giving birth, and lo and behold they experienced a shedload of pain.

I actually got pregnant when I was forty-three and, to be honest, it was a bit of a breeze especially considering I was an elderly primigravida, which is Latin for Quite an Old Lady Having a Baby (i.e. over thirty-six – well past it). I was on tour when I was pregnant the first time, didn't want to tell anyone and my long-term tour manager let me down at the last minute, necessitating my husband Bernie tour-managing for me. And I think that's enough about that already.

Thankfully, I didn't really get any of the traditional pregnancy symptoms. I was already fat, so no one noticed I was pregnant. Bonus! I didn't get morning sickness apart from the time I was off my face on vodka a few weeks in ... kidding. I was tired but that was okay, I've been tired since I was about twenty. Other than that it was unremarkable really. Hadn't quite emotionally catered for the terror every little twinge would ignite, but I presumed that went with the territory.

The press sent me a bunch of flowers a week before I gave birth saying 'Congratulations'. The press getting something wrong? How unusual.

The hospital was fine, though I did have a slightly weird encounter with a nurse who really hurt me when she gave me an injection. When I remonstrated and an unpreventable swear word slipped out, she asked, 'Can I kiss it better?' Not sure which nursing manual that's in.

To be honest I was pretty impressed my forty-three-year-old body managed it twice without too much trouble and as someone who smoked until my late thirties, drank like a fish till I was thirty-five and obviously carried too much weight, in many ways it was a bloody miracle. But, obviously, I am not recommending this approach to you.

The Menopause

Apparently women in Japan don't really have a menopause. If only we could work out why then everything would be good over in the West. Is it the fish? Is it the soya? Is it the kimonos? I have to say that the menopause was pretty mild for me or maybe I'm a trouper who just trudges on regardless of setbacks.

I didn't really have any hot flushes, though I was quite grumpy but that was par for the course. The other issue of course is dryness but I never used to think about the weather much. Did you really think I was going to go there?

It is at this stage that many women decide to go ahead with HRT (I have my own form of this, Haribo Replacement Therapy: this is when I eat all the kids' sweets and I know they will find out). I decided against HRT after seeing Teresa Gorman discussing it on the news and thinking she'd turned into a Les Dawson drag character.

If I Said You Had a Beautiful Body . . .

So, women's bodies are scrutinised more than ever and a standard that is not quite reached in reality is easily airbrushed to produce the perfect woman, and then young women think they have to look like that. Older women think they have to stay like that. Thankfully a lot of women ignore this but many don't and suffer torment over features that are not quite right.

And the fact of the matter is that men go stupid over beautiful women, but who wants a silly arse that does that? Not me. (Just as well, I hear you snigger.) Neurosis has exploded owing to the plethora of websites illustrating how 'acceptable' women look. And although recently the concept of 'fat-shaming' has appeared, the blokes who would shout abuse at fat women probably still do as long as there aren't any armed feminists around.

We've come a long way and in many areas of life women are no longer judged on their appearance ... and that's why *Love Island* is so popular.

My generation experimented with quite a lot of different forms of make-up from the pale-lipped sixties, which made you look slightly like a walking corpse, to the melodrama of punk, or the bright turquoise-eyelidded kohl-eyelinered *Top of the Pops* devotee. My daughters' generation appear to be permanently decorating their bodies with tattoos, some of them going all the way up to the jawline, blokes in particular, and it just looks like they've got creeping green neck acne to me. People always say, 'Ooh, what's that going to look like when they're old?' Shrivelled, presumably, like all of us, apart from the ones who've laid their faces on a stretching machine.

Body Hair

Body hair has likewise become a complete obsession. When I was young, eyebrows were plucked to within an inch of their lives (think David Bowie at his Ziggy Stardust peak or Dora from *Follyfoot* farm); now they have become vast bushy strips that Frida Kahlo might have been perturbed by. But any other kind of body hair is a complete no-no. It also seems that most women, who have obviously been sent the memo, now have absolutely no pubic hair left at all – the inspiration, I believe, has to be porn films. And I suppose to some extent that it makes women look pre-pubescent. Sounds pervy, doesn't it? And it probably is.

I had hoped that the battle of the sexes would be over by now and that women would be as tolerant and relaxed about their bodies as men are. We all appreciate male beauty but let's be honest: for men a kind demeanour and a sense of humour have long proved perfectly acceptable, cancelling out a peeping beer gut, troll's feet, a spotty bum and a not-very-attractive face. Not so in the case of women.

Alas, though, it's gone totally the other way. Men now worry, scrub, moisturise, deodorise, dress carefully, diet, go to the gym and WORRY, like only women, posh blokes and gay men once did.

Why has this happened and why is being obsessed with the outward appearance of our bodies one of the few battles that women have won? I suspect that money is at the root of this. Just think how much more companies believe they can make from persuading men to buy manly cosmetic products, tastefully designed in black, even if the reality is (according to Mumsnet) that lots of OHs – I think that means husbands – are borrowing their wives' moisturiser, shower gel and tweezers. Oh well, a fond adieu to nose hair can only be a good thing.

3

YOU ARE NOT WHAT YOU WEAR

Dungarees and Doc Martens? That's not a feminist, that's a plumber.

In 2002 when my younger daughter was about six months old I took part in a TV show called *What Not to Wear* with Trinny Woodall and Susannah Constantine, which had been pencilled in but not confirmed, because I was taking part in a Comic Relief show called *Fame Academy*. The stars must have been aligned as I was chucked off *Fame Academy* by an audience vote the day before I was due to start *What Not to Wear*. I had banked on my voice not taking me far. In their defence, Trinny and Susannah gave my TV career a real boost. I had been out of circulation for a while on maternity leave and it really catapulted me back into the limelight.

Now let's take the show apart, brick by brick.

If you didn't see Trinny and Susannah, young person, they got members of the public in a vice-like grip, slagged off their clothes and then made them wear the clothes they thought would suit them. Their comments were often acidic and mean-spirited but then again that makes for brilliant telly, doesn't it?

On the whole Susannah was the good policeman and Trinny the bad and when I was asked, along with Sophie Raworth, the newsreader, to do the show, which would be an attempt to make us look decent on the red carpet at the BAFTAs, I agreed. I knew they would do their best to humiliate me. I was not expecting much as I didn't like the way either of them dressed. Susannah always looked like she had been upholstered by Cath Kidston and Trinny's clothes suggested a cross between Joanna Lumley in *The New Avengers* and an Eastern European dictator on his way to a party.

Their first insult was that I looked like a man. Well, that made me suicidal ... not ... and it went from there with them taking me shopping to department stores and showing me a selection of matronly big-lady clothes that would have gone down a treat at the Tory Party Conference. At one point, one of them tried to pull my leggings down for a hilarious glimpse of a continent of cellulite and they also sent me into a room with 360-degree mirrors dressed only in a size zero leotard, while I was forced to turn like a turkey on a vertical spit as they critiqued my unacceptable shape. They claimed, however, that they had discovered my waist – hilarious – and focused on an outfit that would show it off. So they ended up selecting a brown (brown?) two-piece combo consisting of a sort of bolero jacket and a long skirt and then a top that showed off some cleavage. (Yuk, I hate cleavage and I find something unpleasant about it no matter what age women are. It makes me think of Page 3 and Nell Gwynn, both of which are all about showing your frontage off to men – something I never felt moved to do.)

I was also forced into a cubicle at the Queen's ex-bra suppliers, Rigby and Peller, to be measured up by a fearsome-looking woman with a hint of an Austrian accent, who upon gazing at my naked top half said, 'Hmm, not as bad as I'd imagined.' (Can I just reassure you, this moment was not caught on camera.) And of course Her Maj is always the look I try to go for.

Suffice to say, it was a surreal experience. I parried Trinny and Susannah's blows as best I could, but the fact is I really didn't give a shit what they thought and I do not like the way women are humiliated into feeling they look wrong. Do what you like, women! Wear what you want. The male gaze is going to be similar whatever you've got on: i.e. if you're dressed like a stripper that doesn't make men rape you.

I am a bit weird about clothes, because I don't really like them much and I can't be bothered with them. That doesn't mean that I want to wander round with nothing on, God forbid – it's simply that I used to feel a lot of pressure to decide what I should wear and how I should keep up with everybody else. Being a fat person doesn't help either, because although there is a recent movement that encourages fat people refusing to be fat-shamed and to wear whatever they want – good for them –I am pre-fat-shaming and I like wearing sacks.

*

I must have read somewhere in a magazine hundreds of years ago that wearing black makes you look thinner and I've always been a bit of a closet goth as well. Dressed mostly in black I am the obvious choice for the Me Too campaign and I was heartened to see that so many women have taken my lead to protest about something that I have been going on about for my entire bloody life.

Once you've found your colour, fair enough, move on, but then the problem I had is that I don't like having to choose articles of clothing, even though there is obviously a huge array of styles, even in black.

I have a friend who if she finds something she likes to wear buys six of them and then doesn't go shopping for ages. I have a very similar approach: I don't buy six, but I will probably buy three. So if you've seen me on programmes like *Have I Got News for You* wearing colours that is not my choice; it is someone else's, because for some reason telly people don't want me to wear black all the time. They make me wear flowery things that I personally think make me look like a middle-aged tubby shrub. I think media people have tried to control women's image far more than men's over the years and this is because the magic of television in many producers' eyes is all about looking as lamby as possible and ruling out the muttony side of my dress sense.

I'm not so worried about it that I dig my heels in and say, 'No, I insist on wearing black.' I am quite happy to put on what someone gives me, I just can't be bothered to go and get it myself. I know people buy shirts for the men on shows such as *Have I Got News* and the element of choice is there occasionally, but I have been left in no doubt that colours are preferable and sometimes I feel sorry for the poor wardrobe person with seventeen flowery colourful tops and one black one, trying to wrestle it off me.

Recently I attended a film premiere and for once, I thought, I'll try and wear something a bit smart. There was a charming picture in the MailOnline, (which someone helpfully pointed out to me), describing my long black dress as 'billowing', like I was the lead ship in the Spanish Armada. That is the thing: you cannot get away with it if you are going to public events. When I went to the BAFTAs wearing a sort of tartany top, someone wrote: 'Jo Brand looks hideous in tartan.' So?

I saw a photo of Patti Smith not so long ago going to the Oscars, I think it was, wearing filthy old jeans and a man's jacket and cowboy boots. Good on yer, Patti.

Now some men choose to believe, and they vocalise this, that women who don't want to spend a fortune on clothes are in fact lesbians, because if they were heterosexuals they would want to go out and spend a lot of money looking nice to please men.

No one ever asks men who they are dressing for. Men's clothes are on the whole pretty drab. Are they dressing for the Grim Reaper? Also, if a man tries to be a bit quirky by wearing, say, red trousers, that just makes everyone feel a bit queasy and think he's a knob. Do men dress for other men? Quite frankly, my dear, who gives a damn?

One often hears that women are dressing for other women. Who are they then? I'm dressing for Mary Beard and Rihanna. I hope they both like the black leggings and black T-shirt I've got on today. Sorry, I can't take this seriously.

There is a difference, I suppose, between whether women dress elegantly for other women and sexily for men. However, I feel so removed from questions of this kind, which I think is why I've been perceived as a man-hater in the past because I can't answer these questions sensibly. Bear in mind this is what I'd call 'dressing up' so I can't take it seriously enough to do it like a grown-up lady. So I can't take it seriously enough to do it. To me, it's the equivalent of little girls' dressing-up boxes full of tiaras, feather boas and stuff that glitters. Most women don't have the luxury of elegance or sex during their day. There's a real mix of different types of women who simply can't be arsed to dress up. That's me and may I add to that, that whenever I am dressed nicely, I cannot keep clean. Inevitably a huge lump of curry comes flying through the air from nowhere and splats on my clothes. My worst challenge ever would be to wear a white suit the whole day and not come home looking like a Jackson Pollock.

A List of Clothes That Are Comfortable

Big pants, baggy T-shirts, leggings, flat shoes.

A List of Clothes That Make You Feel Uncomfortable

Euphemistically named 'shapewear', body-hugging dresses, pencil skirts, cleavage-revealing tops, an article of clothing that is just sleeves that old women can put under sleeveless tops so people don't have to be upset by the sight of their old lady arms, ridiculously high shoes.

The Difference?

Comfy clothes LET IT ALL HANG OUT.

More formal clothes and shoes CONSTRAIN YOU. They are really irritating to wear and you can't walk properly, and that's what I call putting women in their place (i.e. not able to move or run away).

Uniforms

Uniforms can be a mixed blessing; they identify you as the member of a work, fan or political group, say like a police officer. This is a dubious signifier depending on whether you are at the station Christmas party or the Notting Hill Carnival.

Uniforms start quite early for children, sometimes at nursery. They enable you to be spotted in case you wander off from the gang, but they also tie you to an ethos. Schoolkids tend to reject or customise their uniforms. I think the general rule is the smarter the uniform, the posher the kid. Of course skirts climb up as a gesture of defiance. If only schoolgirls really knew the sort of man who would find this attractive, they wouldn't do it.

I actually went to a grammar school that was twenty-five miles away from my home so had to endure a two-and-a-half-hour journey each way. I'm afraid to say we had hats, felt ones in winter and straw ones in summer, which made us look like female gondoliers. Our biggest protest was not wearing our hats all the time on the bus, so occasionally a teacher would be stationed on the outskirts of town to see who was and wasn't offending. At least she didn't catch us smoking crack.

Of course, the upside of having uniforms, especially at school, is that it doesn't matter how wealthy your parents are, everybody looks the same. No gold-plated Nikes or designer jeans, the democracy of uniform takes over. It's rather liberating just having to put on the same things every day judging by the torturous amount of time some of my friends spend trying to decide what to wear.

My charming editor has suggested here that I talk about some of my favourite pieces of clothing. Hahahahaha! I can barely remember the clothes I wore last week so here are some weird clothes-related stories that stand out.

When I was a teenager I went out with an Italian boy for the summer. For my birthday he bought me a really horrible chain belt and I'm afraid I chucked him. Sorry, Claudio.

I have a pair of boots with steel toecaps that I have had since 1992, given to me as a present after I compered a charity fashion show at Loughborough University. They are quite scary-looking and look as if I have polished the steel toecaps on assorted testicles that got in my way. They were already like that, chaps, I have kicked not one single bollock in those boots. However I remain superstitious about those boots and have worn them on every TV show I have ever done just about. I was once persuaded to do a TV pilot panel-show-type thing with a pair of proper lady shoes with quite high heels. I had to totter down some stairs at the start of the show; it looked ridiculous and unsurprisingly that show was not commissioned.

When I was at university I was miserable because I'd just been dumped by someone who, looking back, wasn't all that. However, I was almost paralysed with grief and throughout the ensuing few months I knitted myself a pink fluffy jumper, which looked shit when I had finished it. But that jumper has so much emotion and pain in its stitches, it's kind of my version of the Turin Shroud.

I did have some lucky pants but they were confiscated by the council.

Style-wise I don't really have any fashion icons apart from Terry Jones in Monty Python's occasional forays into cross-dressing – particularly in *The Meaning of Life* during the unforgettable musical number, 'Every Sperm Is Sacred'.

I suppose the only fashions I followed were in my teenage years when I was a part-time hippy: long Laura Ashley skirts, bell-sleeved T-shirts and bare feet. In fact my friend Halcyon's mum got so pissed off with me going round there without a bra on, she actually bought me one and that was when I hardly had any bosoms.

*

A lot of women will say they express themselves through their clothes and certainly clothes do tell you a great deal about a woman. They can more or less tell you their age, they tell you their class, the amount of money they have to throw at clothes and whether they should have gone to Specsavers. Very easy to spot women who are arty or businesslike. Maybe not quite so easy to spot a zoo keeper as it is not obligatory for them to wear gorilla costumes.

When was a teenager in the 1970s, the term 'jailbait' tended to be used for teenagers who were dressed in a sexually provocative way – and that term does not bear too much exploration. Also people often remarked that a woman was dressed like a prostitute, obviously for wearing a short skirt or showing a lot of cleavage.

Similarly in the seventies, someone would call you a lesbian if you had dungarees on or if you were wearing Doc Martens; that was par for the course, and women who were wearing unusual clothes would get abuse on the street about being mad.

I was once heckled on stage in Leeds because my trousers were a bit short. Someone shouted out, 'Why don't you put some jam on your shoes and invite your trousers to tea?' This was so lovely and made everyone laugh so much that I decided not to try and top it with one of my personality-shattering put-downs.

Class and Clothes

Clothes can act as straitjackets for women, because they are apt to be representative of the control that certain cultures or workplaces have over those women. In terms of class, these days people are shamed if they wear what are known as leisure suits, in other words tracky bottoms and a top in a velour-type material. Women in these sorts of clothes tend to be shamed for being 'chavs', which is a word I have always abhorred, because it has become a very strong judgement on someone's supposed class. If someone chooses to go to the shop to get milk in their dressing gown, they too are a chav. We judge people on how much they spend, which shop they've been to, how close to six stone they are hovering and what percentage of the time they look like they are just about to attend a film premiere.

But let's just say that expensive high-end fashion is for extraordinarily thin women that none of us can hope to emulate, and a lot of fairly liberal publications are quite hypocritical in the sense that in their letters pages or in their leader columns women are continually speaking out against the fashion industry, and yet you still see models in their fashion sections whose arms are about as wide as one of my big toes.

These days there is a bit more of a choice clothes-wise, although unfortunately the choice is displayed by what is known as a plus-size model. There's something about that demeaning phrase that puts you off buying anything worn by a 'plus-size model'. I'm sorry, but could they not call these (mainly) women something nicer? It is getting more acceptable to be bigger, I suppose, although there's a constant battle against us, with the NHS now telling us that we portly types are the new cancer, or the new

44

alcoholics, or the new drug-users. So we chubbs are getting very mixed messages out there and it is a difficult thing to negotiate, especially if you have to go past a Greggs while you are investigating.

Pink is for Girls

The thing about clothes when I was growing up, particularly for girl children, young and adult women, is that they were used to denote femininity from a very early age. I know it's a massive cliché, but not so long ago babies always used to be dressed in pink or blue, and God forbid if someone dressed their girl in blue: you would have them sectioned under the Mental Health Act. These days it's a little more forgiving, because we have a choice of slightly more colours. When I had my children, Mothercare sold only pink, blue or green, so if you dressed your child in green, that immediately said to people, 'I refuse to label my child,' therefore 'I'm a bit politically left-wing and new-agey and probably a vegetarian,' and then you did truly become an outcast from society.

These days baby clothes are so much more varied, interesting, international and expensive, and they are also what I call TNTVO – too nice to vomit on. People spend a fortune on buying baby clothes that their baby is going to grow out of within weeks, literally. We all love the look of a tiny little pair of flowery DMs, but, God, they do not fit the little blighters after a couple of weeks, so it is as utterly pointless as throwing your money down the toilet.

When I was younger, one custom I thought was lovely was the knitting that your grandma did to make things for the grandchildren. That's pretty rare these days and I think it's a shame, because baby clothes knitted by your grandma were totally personal and something to cherish and keep. That's exactly what I have done, because my grandma knitted lots of clothes for us as kids, and later for my children as well, as their great-grandma, and they're all sitting in a box somewhere, ready for me to get out when I'm really old and have a little cry to.

Once babies became children back then, it was very obvious what they were: if they were a little girl, they wore a sort of gingham dress, pastel colours, or a skirt and a nice blouse. Apart from that tiny group of girls, of which I was a member, called 'tomboys', which covered a whole raft of different attitudes towards clothes – the revolutionary, the can't-be-bothered, the action girl – which all came under that heading. Whereas shoes pretty much came under two headings: Clarks if you were posh and plimsolls if you weren't posh, as they were an awful lot cheaper.

I think clothes for little girls nowadays have set them back, because of their girliness. Lots of them are simply miniature versions of garments that adults would wear. I remember seeing Suri Cruise, who is Tom Cruise's little girl, in a photo on her sixth birthday, wearing high heels, and I thought, Hmm, she's not really the one in that family who needs to wear heels, is she?

There are also the branded items, with slogans on, which are sometimes worn inappropriately by very young girls. I saw a six-year-old once at a party, and she had a top that said 'Foxy Lady' on it. That's a bit weird, isn't it? Presumably she ran around at night making an awful noise and eating food out of the bins, but I never did check up on that.

As girls get older, a new category has been invented for them – it is so exciting – that recognises that period between A GIRL and A TEENAGER and that is a 'tween-ager'. Tweenagers have their own brand of cutesy, yet not-quite-grown-up-enough-to-wear-a-bra-type outfits, which I'm going to gloss over, because I don't want to give big business any more of a nod than I have to.

Once girls become teenagers, certainly when I was growing up, they take more risks. Dads all over the country sigh and shout after their daughters as they go out in very short skirts. In my day what you did was to wait until you got down the road and then hoick your skirt up and throw your nun's outfit in the bin – obviously the best way to approach that problem.

These days, shoes, bags and clothes are tribal for many girls. You stick with a brand that you admire and so does the rest of your group, so in many ways you all look exactly the same. You need to have the latest thing, or the latest brand of bag, and you must have the right trainers on. We used to have plimsolls that cost about £1.50 – now the trainers that girls want to wear start at about £100, and that seems a huge amount to me; and they're not even using them for training in.

As far as clothes for adults are concerned, once you are able to choose exactly what you want to wear, you decide on what you like and you tend to stick with it. So you've got the adults who want to look younger, who go to Topshop and places like that, or the adults who want to look like they mean business, who might go to Marks & Spencer's and buy a nice suit. As women creep towards middle age, the glorious attitude of 'couldn't care less' is welcomed into their life, apart from the ones whose lips have been inflated beyond reasonable doubt.

I assume that my not-giving-a-shit attitude about clothes, which marks me out from my friends and my daughters, originates from two incidents to do with fire.

First, I was caught coming out of *Last Tango in Paris* with seven men by my parents when I was roughly fifteen years old and had seriously messed up on the alibi front. My dad, whose anger could be flamboyant and over the top, drove me home, went straight up to my bedroom, cleared all my drawers (furniture not knickers) and the wardrobe of every shred of patchouli-soaked rag I owned and built a bonfire in the garden with them, and then poured petrol on and set fire to them. At least I wasn't in the clothes.

My mum then replaced my 'hippy rags' with several sets of 'sensible' skirts and blouses. I even hate the fucking word 'blouse' – it conjures up lavender-smelling compliance to me.

And then, some years later when I lived in a bedsit in Tunbridge Wells, I burned my flat down and once again lost every piece of clothing I had. I think at that point unconsciously I resolved never to be that bothered with what I wore and I never have been since. But I have found it by turns sweet and hilarious to observe people trying to feminise me – one suspects it'll get pretty chilly in hell first. So take it from me – you are NOT what you wear.

4

BEING DIFFERENT

I've got a deep voice so I always get called 'sir' on the phone and occasionally in the flesh too.

Watching groups of girls come out of school underlines the way that girls tend to categorise themselves socially. The various gangs are wearing a uniform within a uniform, be it long hair, too much make-up, skirts hitched up in an identical way, shoes exactly the same. The sleek, tall low-weighters have a slightly 'we're special!' demeanour that marks these young women out as 'popular girls', while those with glasses, scurrying about and looking apologetic about the space they're occupying, tend to be the geeks; all the other tribes fall in between with varying shades of popularity or geekiness. To be unable to conform to the requirements of *the group* at school is a very painful condition and occupies the minds and hearts of many as they make their way through the stressful process of trying to be accepted.

Then again, on the other hand, so much advertising and advice is about *being you*, whatever that may mean.

Conform, but shine individually . . . sums up the concept of cognitive dissonance and is not really possible, so I just decided to go for the individual bit.

I always felt like I was a bit different, but I'm struggling to explain why that was. The nearest explanation I can give is that I was a kind of tomboy hermaphrodite hetero sexual. Throughout my life many people have assumed I'm a lesbian or all points in between. I'm not in the slightest bit interested in clothes, I have short hair and occasionally sound off about the shortcomings of the male gender, but I like flowers, *Love Island* and nail varnish. Yes, it's that easy to mark someone out as coming from a particular tribe, especially if you're from a tabloid newspaper. I know that when I started doing stand-up, my lack of femininity and my gobbiness were very much to the forefront of any comment about my work. Of course the reality is we're forever being forced into boxes marked 'That's What You Are' and if we try and crawl out of them it makes some people's brains melt.

As you get older you care less, but the pain about not being included in a group is still very raw, as attested to by many poignant posts on Mumsnet from grown-up women who have been left out of weekends away, meeting up for coffee or whose child has not been invited to a party: it still stings. As a mother you just want to go round and hit the offending parent with a baseball bat, but so far I have managed to contain myself.

Thankfully I have also managed to steer clear of school reunions. I feel that I have kept in touch with the people from school that I want to see and I don't particularly want to play the game of Who Turned Out to be a Failure. That floats some people's boats – it sinks mine. Failure is such a subjective judgement anyway. I always thought that Friends Reunited, an early website on the internet, which got people all flustered as they pursued old flames from school, was a bit risky.

I think quite a few people broke up marriages to pursue the mirage of their first love who had in reality metamorphosed into a bad-tempered, beer-bellied bastard or a narky old harridan with nicotine-stained grey hair. Friends Reunited sadly faded away eventually like the hope of a generation for new love.

I had always been pretty well behaved and uncontroversial, then we moved, and suddenly I was uprooted from a school I really loved to one I didn't really want to be at. I had begged my mum and dad to let me travel in every day or stay the week with a friend but they were unbending. So I went to Hastings High School, where I was immediately drawn towards the other rebels and fairly quickly began to skive off school and sit in a café smoking my head off with fellow school-avoiders.

Hastings was buzzing with hundreds of foreign students in the summer, holidaymakers, brilliant bands on the pier, T. Rex among them, and it was all very exciting. Most people my age gathered in the Old Town, a quaint area of narrow streets and pubs and a dodgy nightclub called the Aquarius. Looking back and now being the mother of teenage daughters, I realise how much I must have driven my mum and dad mad with worry, but I was selfish, felt hard done by and determined; it was grim for all sides.

I felt a million miles apart from my parents; my dad was always angry and my mum hardly there because she was working so hard. Had either side given the other a bit of slack, maybe it would have been easier, but there was a complete lack of trust. Maybe if the following had been tried . . .

What Worked/Would Have Worked

- Non-judgemental invitations to talk about areas of disagreement.
- Compromise: 'You can go to X party but . . . home by eleven/twelve etc., etc.' They were always very rigid in their proclamations.
- Offering a viable alternative: 'No, you can't tout for business on the seafront but how about a new piece of clothing/some music instead?'
- Allowing me to invite friends on trips.
- My mum keeping my dad, at his angriest, away from me.
- Letting my brother keep an eye on me when out.
- My mum supporting me now and again in an argument. My dad's verbal attacks were so biased.
- Not trying to make me read Jane Austen.
- Not tutting during *Top of the Pops* and saying, 'I can't understand a word.' (I know this is a HUGE cliché, but my dad really did that.)

What Didn't Work At All

- Moving me from a school that I really loved and was working hard at, to a place where I knew no one.
- Shouting at me.

- Keeping me in.
- Hitting me.
- Burning my clothes, then buying me new ones from M&S.
- Slagging off my friends.
- Expressing wild uninformed fears about drugs.
- Saying things like, 'You must meet the local vicar's daughter; perhaps you'd get on really well.'

My dad was in a really bad way, and my mum was struggling to cope. Then I fell madly in love with a posh, unemployed heroin addict (see 'How Not to Fall in Love' for more on this) who drank like a fish. After my dad had knocked him out a couple of times, I was given the choice of continuing to see him and leaving home, or forgetting about him and being welcomed back. Much to their horror, or relief, I was never sure, I jumped at the chance to leave home.

I accept that up to this point I was hellish to deal with. I was always angry, sneaking out, getting drunk – I was god-awful really. I do accept that. I think my dad's tolerance was really low because of his poor mental health. My parents were desperate and didn't know what to do. So, aged sixteen, I moved into a bedsit on my own – and took over responsibility for my life. And it was bloody great. After years of being told what to do – turn your music down, don't dress like that – suddenly being able to do what you want is so wonderful. Cereal in the middle of the night, wine on your porridge . . . I was the Queen of Independent Living and revelled in the hippy, dippy environment where everyone seemed so chilled.

I wanted to be an actor but as a sixteen-year-old living in a bedsit in Hastings with no money, I had to work. I was in this bedsit in a tall Victorian house overlooking the sea, a madhouse with a Rastafarian, Eric, above me, above him many Korean chefs in one room, below me a grandma who sold cannabis and below her her daughter, a single mum with a mixed-race baby, an absolute scandal in those days in Hastings. It was a bit like a play at the Royal Court, home of scandalous and frequently unpalatable drama. I often played cards all night with the chefs, who would cook lovely food and tut a lot at the fact that I was so young and living on my own. Eric the Rasta would give me ready-rolled joints and Sally and I would often have tea in the afternoon when the baby was asleep.

I painted my room bright red and blue, not realising there were different types of paint, so of course thought the walls were shiny because the paint was wet. After two weeks I had to admit I'd bought gloss.

I had a ridiculous out-of-control life back then: all my friends were at school or at home, behaving themselves, getting up in the morning, putting on the uniform, and I loved it – right till the moment I went to meet the reason I had been thrown out of home in the pub to find him snogging someone else in the corner.

The idea of comedy began to form in my head but I had no idea what the career path was, so convinced myself that doing a degree and becoming a nurse was the next best thing. Then slowly (over several years) the pull of stand-up comedy became stronger. There's more on how that happened in 'How to Do What You Want' so I won't blah on here about it. But with comedy I felt like I'd finally found my home.

No one becomes a comedian because they feel like they completely fit in to the world they come from. And what's more, it means you can actually make a living from doing material about the mismatch between you and your environment. Having met many comedians over the years, I'd say there does seem to be a common thread that holds them together as a group, which I would loosely describe as 'family disturbance'. Under this heading comes losing a parent young, being adopted, parents being alcohol- or drug-users, parents with mental health problems or violent parents. Often, being bullied at school is cited as being the common thread among comedians but I would imagine the 'otherness' that resulted in them being bullied was the seed of comedy in them.

I have never been bullied by other kids but I have been bullied by teachers and I have had a lot of abuse in my life – and I have seen women around me get far worse. I was brought up in a feminist household and yet my childhood was overshadowed by the fear of my dad's rages. I think a lot of my material comes out of that relief in being an adult at last and being able to answer back and to talk about the things, whether it's periods or weight or unsatisfactory men, that girls aren't expected to talk about. It's funny that men are encouraged to 'speak their minds' but when women do it, it's seen as 'being lippy'.

Difference and non-conformity have always been frowned upon by some of society, who in a very primitive way find themselves disturbed by it. So in this group we can include those of different racial origin and sexuality who have long been discriminated against and still are covertly, despite increasing amounts of legislation in place to prevent it.

It goes without saying that the ruling class is still primarily white, privileged and male and there are constant reminders that being different – whether in race, gender or sexuality – makes you in some way inferior. I'm sure at some point humans will stop being led by ignorance and superstition but until that time we need to be vigilant. I used to get the word lesbian thrown at me a lot as an intended insult and always used to say (because it was always by a man), 'Well I am now I've seen you.'

In my day sexuality was fairly simple, gay or straight, but the march of the years has brought ever more complex divisions of sexual preference, some of which I constantly have to ask my daughters about. They roll their eyes and look at me as if I am a dinosaur – and that's even when I don't even have my dinosaur costume on.

I do not profess to be an expert on the aforementioned so I am not going to force-feed you my probably adolescent views on sexuality.

Suffice to say from experience among my friends:

- It's still not easy in some places so be aware of your safety.
- If you're stressing about coming out to your parents, rest assured most of them will already know.
- If you can't bear to tell your parents for whatever reason – don't.

We've come a long way since the Brontë sisters had to pretend to be men to get their novels published, but that was the 1860s. However, not far enough as a number of women writers still use either initials or a male name so you can't tell what gender they are, so they must think there is some advantage. What about Lionel Shriver? I'd have preferred Sam. No one should have to pretend to be something they're not any more, although we all know there are leading men in Hollywood who are gay and won't come out, and it shocked me recently to hear at the Commonwealth Games that out of the fifty-three countries competing, thirty-six criminalise homosexuality. Can't Her Maj sort that?

Once you've decided who and what you are, then you have to try and like yourself for it. Easier said than done of course. I have two out of three positive advantages in society today. I'm white and I'm educated. Just need to have a sex change now. Watch this space!

5

WHY FRIENDS ARE SO IMPORTANT

A friend is someone who can tell you you look like Brian
Blessed in drag – in a nice way.

What makes a good friend? Well, in my book, it is someone you can trust, someone who's a good laugh, someone
who's interesting, someone who doesn't endlessly moan
to you about a horrible boyfriend and then carry on seeing
them, someone who is non-judgemental, someone who's
fun, someone who has roughly the same politics as you,
someone who never says 'I told you so', someone who
doesn't criticise you or remark on negative aspects of your
personality (unless you're a serial killer, obviously), someone who you can say anything to, someone who puts up
with you when you're being a pain in the arse, someone
who doesn't feel threatened by you, or you don't feel
threatened by, and someone who is simply an all-round,
caring, kind, reliable person.

I have three best friends, Betty, Helen[*] and Edana; yes, an oxymoron to some extent. We met at university, all of us doing social sciences and work placements in the summer. Three of us trained as mental health nurses while the fourth, Betty, had decided on a career in clinical psychology and worked in the appropriate areas for that job. I don't want to list their individual qualities not least because they will be going through this with a fine-tooth comb, but they are all very bright, have brilliant senses of humour, are interested in everything and all have ambitions that are sincerely held but not ferocious and will drop anything to come and help.

Sometime during our student nursing years I was in a very intense short relationship. I was in thrall to him and thought it was all going really well. One day, completely out of the blue, he finished the relationship, and I plunged down a deep dark well that I thought I would never scramble out of. I called Helen (geographically nearest at the time) and she appeared immediately, despite the fact that yes, I had completely neglected her and the others to moon about in a psychotic bubble of love for months, pretty much entirely forgetting their existence. Helen took control of the situation, whisked me off to the pub fairly early in the day and we got absolutely rat-arsed, possibly not the most sensible, but definitely the most effective solution for that day, and the resulting hangover turned the next few days into a hazy bridge to the land of surviving and

---

[*] Sadly Helen, or 'Griffo', died at the end of June 2018, but I didn't want to erase her from the triumvirate.

re-building. And never once was my physical absence from the friendship mentioned.

For many people, friends are the new family. A lot of people I know have replaced their disliked/unmanageable/toxic/interfering family with their friends. Because it goes without saying that to many, families are a disappointment that we are stuck with for many years before we can escape.

But the friends thing hasn't worked for everyone: if we look at British society today, a huge proportion of people say they are lonely. Friendship is very difficult to nurture and one has to have give-and-take: if it's all take, then those relationships start to fall apart.

For me, the most important point about lasting friendship is that you need to make an effort to maintain it. I think that people who are lonely don't do that. I'm sorry, people out there who are lonely and who are probably seething at me now and going, 'Yes we do, and we have done, but it's not our fault – it's other people's fault.'

Let's start at the beginning with friendships. I don't think that very young children are quite sophisticated enough to form very close bonds with other kids, probably until the age of seven or eight. They tend to play in parallel rather than together. There are obviously some children who are thrown together by the proximity of their parents' friendships, and provided they are not ripping the other child's eyes out, the parents will smile fondly and say, 'Oh, aren't they good friends,' but I don't believe that is what's happening. It's called 'convenience'.

I had a double whammy, friendship-wise, with school mums: because I was an older mother and because everyone seemed so much younger than me at the school gates, our points of reference were very different. I was always ready to 'woman' the barricades in the feminist war, whereas 'some of them' seemed more of the Girl Power generation. Has there ever been a more misguided campaign attempting to give women more power by calling them 'girls'? Added to that there were a lot of people who would tell me that our children were friends when they barely knew each other, because I was on the telly. Also, there were mums who were at pains to point out, in one way or another, that I wasn't quite as great as I thought I was, without even checking whether I thought I was great in the first place, which I didn't.

One thing that parents think they can do, but can't, is manipulate their offspring's friendships and this is something I found it hard to deal with, particularly if I didn't like the friend or thought they were being hurtful to one of my kids. The Machiavellian side of you just has to bite your tongue while the children gingerly make their way through the friendship maze. No one can bear to see their child being hurt but the rules are that you don't slag off someone else's child even if they've behaved really badly. This should change, in my opinion, but the fact remains that the vast majority of parents have angelic goggles on when they look at their children and criticising them evokes a furious response, however you deliver the news.

Still, I suppose if they have real friends that is an improvement on imaginary ones. In my family, my little brother Matt was the only one with imaginary friends. His friends were two little boys called Cady and Vraymond ... yes, I've no idea either. Their main job seemed to be to take the rap for minor criminal offences my brother had committed. Who took the sweets out of the cupboard? That'll have been Cady. Who put all the woodlice under your pillow? Why, none other than that naughty Vraymond!

In primary school, friendships are often based on a queen-bee type orchestrating the different levels of friends that are buzzing around her; or individual children, either having the sophistication to be a puppet master and control the other kids, or having something attractive about them that other kids are drawn to – like chocolate.

So, friendships at that age can be shallow and based on fairly arbitrary concepts, such as living next door, or liking that person's pet, or them being the only person who will talk to you.

Once children become more socialised out of the home, and start to grow up, they realise that their family is a ragtag bunch of risible half human beings and that friend-ship is the best way forward. Friendship etiquette, however, is very much controlled by one's experience in the family home. If there's a good model for friendship in your family – treating people with respect, trusting people, not hitting them, that kind of thing – then you will probably be pretty good at making friends. Whereas if you are a child who lives in a difficult family, where maybe there are alcohol problems or communication is skewed in some other way, then when you are sent out into the world you could find it really hard to understand the rules of friendship.

I think the most essential elements of conducting a friendship are:

Your old mate 'Low Expectations': by this I don't mean any old person who wanders within a ten-metre radius of you can be your friend, but rather, don't have expectations that are too high. There is no friend out there who is the perfect combo of Holly Willoughby, Mother Teresa, Zoella, Beyoncé and Meghan Markle (God forbid), so bear in mind everyone has flaws and you have to be prepared to accept them for the friendship to work. You will know how far you are prepared to compromise. Be generous!

Kindness: I come across a lot of people who are unkind and friendship-wise they are a big no-no. Sometimes they're hard to spot because they disguise unkind comments as jokes. Eventually it will hit you like a light-ning bolt that they're not very nice and they probably don't even like you. Those among you who are bold, chal-lenge them. I don't mean, 'Who the fuck do you think you are?' More, 'When you made that joke about me looking like a moose with a dress on, it wasn't really funny and it upset me . . . so who the fuck do you think you are?'

Seriously, try not to launch in with a challenge and give

them a graceful get-out opportunity. Then if it continues you will have to end the friendship.

A Sense of Humour That Chimes with Yours: there's absolutely no point if you don't find the same things funny. Simple as.

Empathy: this is something that some people are unable to do and that's sad because it's very important in a relationship. I doubt someone would get beyond first base with a friendship if they didn't have some kind of empathy.

'Likes' in common: this includes food, holiday destinations, films, TV shows and many others. Compromises can be reached; for example I tend to indulge my love of Russian-language film and the like with the same friend who has done a film course and doesn't look at me like I've lost the plot, which is quite easy to do in a Russian-language film. But if someone likes Jaffa cakes, not only must they be shunned as a friend, they must be thrown into prison.

After the age of eight or nine, there are a lot of other challenges as far as friendship goes. Are you competing for the friendship of a particular individual? Are you being bullied and, if so, are your friends supporting you? Do your parents like your friends? At that age, this has quite a big impact on how your friendship might go.

Over the years, my parents absolutely loathed quite a few of my friends, and when I was younger they could prevent me seeing them. What drove them mad was when I got a bit older and they couldn't do that any more, and because they didn't like my friends when I was a teenager, that made those friends a lot more attractive to me.

What encroaches most upon friendships during the teenage years is the increasing attraction to someone you might fall in love with. One of the problems at this age – and it only gets worse in some ways in your twenties – is the tendency that girls in particular have to exclude everything else from their lives apart from the partner that they are focused on, be that a boy or a girl.

Why does this happen? I have no idea, I am not going to Google it either, but will hazard a guess at the following.

1. Women tend to have much more sociable relationships than men, which are emotional and confessional, and probably have a wider group of friends.
2. Men have fewer friends than women whom they don't see as often as women see their friends, so when a newly formed couple appears, the woman's friends will immediately notice she's not been around, whereas with the man's smaller number of friends whom he sees less frequently, it will take longer to become apparent.
3. I would take a punt that some men don't even tell their friends they have started a new relationship and the first they know of it is when the wedding invitation arrives (tongue in cheek).
4. Yes, I have been guilty of withdrawing from my female circle of friends but more out of embarrassment in case

they thought my boyfriend was a twat. In many cases they were right.

5. Also, I had one very forthright friend who only met a boyfriend of mine once and virtually pinned him to the wall and threatened him with all sorts if he treated me badly. I was horribly embarrassed, he wasn't too pleased either and then it didn't bloody work anyway.

I have never asked any teenage boys about this issue, mainly because most of them don't say much – not to an old harridan like me anyway.

During my teenage years, friends were important to reinforce who I was as a person. My relationship with my parents totally fell apart when I was about fifteen, and therefore the rebel kids I made friends with fulfilled a particular need at that time, but as I have got older, I have tended to have friends who are good at baking and going to the chip shop.

Five Tips on How to Make Friends

1. Be open-minded; don't always look for someone who is within your age range and income bracket. It's nice to have friends from a wider circle and it opens windows on to other worlds.

2. Don't be afraid of being rejected: if you make the first move to be friendly and they look frightened, it's their loss and they're weird.

3. Don't go to evening classes: I've always thought that advice was bollocks. I don't know anyone who met a new friend/partner at evening classes.

4. Join clubs, book clubs, cinema clubs, maybe even a skateboarding club: then you might meet someone in hospital.
5. Be casual: 'Fancy a coffee sometime?' This will work better than, 'I've booked us two weeks in Clacton for a conference on thrush.'

How to Keep Friends

1. Don't have sex with their husbands (or wives).
2. Don't laugh at their new tattoo, even if it's spelled wrong.
3. Try to answer their calls.
4. Don't rifle through their handbag when they're in the toilet.
5. Occasionally buy a round.

Friends as flatmates occasionally ends in tears as you realise that someone who was really good fun before they moved in is in fact a pant-scattering, thin-skinned *Top Gear* fan who goes into a cold sweat when they see dirty dishes. If you value the friendship, move out.

One major issue that impacts upon lasting friendships is that age-old awkward scenario of your friend falling in love with someone and disappearing over the horizon before you can say, 'But I thought we were going clubbing on Saturday.' It has happened to all of us and it is extraordinarily irritating. It's very difficult not to be angry about it, as you sit and wallow in misery, boyfriend- or girlfriend-less, while you know that your best friend is out getting a good seeing-to and you are watching the news and wiping your tears away with salt and vinegar crisps.

It's easy to convince yourself that said friend is being a bit of a twat. Because, let's face it, everyone who is madly in love does seem like a bit of a twat to the outside world. They can't help it really, poor dears. (See my chapter 'How Not to Fall in Love' for more on that.)

What is more annoying than your friend dropping you when they've got a new partner? Well, it's when that partner has given them the elbow and suddenly, hey, they are back in touch again, trying to pretend that they didn't completely drop you for the last few months and, hey, can't everything carry on as normal?

Now in a lot of cases, most of us are only too grateful to receive that person back into the fold, but not before we have made a few sarcastic comments about how long it has been. Then we have to recalibrate our views about the future of our friendship, to take in the fact that the next person they meet may well mean they will bugger off and leave you on your own again. I once deserted most of my friends for a very long period of time when I was a teenager and then when things didn't work out sought them out for some sympathy. A couple of my friends were a bit put out so I tried to convince them I'd been trying to protect them from him because they'd all said they thought he was an arse and I wanted to keep him and them apart. And anyway, eight years isn't such a long time, is it?

As a young adult, this can become a more lasting problem because they might actually marry the bugger. I think this happens a lot especially between best friends and partners. Best friend feels she's been usurped and glowers, partner picks that up and lo and behold the invitations start to drop off. I think if that happens, other than getting a big arbitration company to sort it out with talks, it's much easier to just see your erstwhile friend away from your partner. And if you like winding your partner up, you can make it look like you're having an affair.

Crossing the Line

If you hang around in a group, there always tends to be someone in the group that everyone fancies, and that element of competition can destroy a friendship completely.

I have had a few friends who, for one reason or another, have decided that sleeping with my current boyfriend would be okay. It is a huge test of a friendship, which most times never recovers from it. I have had recourse, after one prolonged period of torture when my current beau just stopped calling and then turned out to be seeing my friend behind my back, to damage some property and to not see that friend again ever. Happy days. That is why trust is so extremely high on the list of friendship requirements, way above stuff like being a laugh, or being helpful, having the same politics or both fancying Jon Snow (the *Channel 4 News* one not the *Game of Thrones* one).

There are a number of people in the business of show who only have friends in the business of show and have left friends from the olden days behind. This is a rather sad scenario and I think is caused by two things: on the part of the old friend maybe some envy, maybe some resentment, and on the part of the person who's been successful a certain amount of being up their own arse-ness.

I have managed to hang on to lots of old friends but they are only allowed to visit me on Tuesday evenings for an hour and they have to bring an expensive gift.

Many people ask me if men and women can really be friends and I tell them to go away or I will call the police. My answer, before the police arrive, is 'Of course they can!' Unless obviously they are young, gorgeous and the woman has uncontrollable sexual urges. I think we'll take as read that most men can manage to rustle up a sexual urge at the drop of a hat.

Lots of women maintain friendships that started at school, but they have a very different quality, because the longer you have known someone, the less exciting they become as your life expands. It's difficult, the battle of new friends against old friends. Old friends are like comfy old sofas, but you've heard all their best stories. New friends are exciting uncharted territory, but a massive personality flaw could be just around the corner.

Friendship tends to get much easier as time goes on, because as we grow more familiar with the partner we were once psychotic about, we need other types of relationships more, particularly friendships by the time your partner becomes the boring old fart you once couldn't imagine them metamorphosing into. Ten or fifteen years into a marriage, you will find a lot of people thinking, Oh God, I've lost all my friends, I'd better try and reel some of them back in to save my social life.

It's so much easier these days reconnecting with old friends. But I would say: be prepared for disappointment. They might be quite happy they haven't seen you for years and you might have forgotten about the two hundred quid you owed them.

The Difference Between Male and Female Friendship

I find there's a huge difference between male and female friendships. Women are much more adept at maintaining friendships through their marriages or their partnerships. My experience tells me that, on the whole, women will have roughly a group of about eight to ten very close friends, whereas men might have only one or two mates that they have maintained all the way through their partnership with someone and their children and that's an optimistic assessment.

Can you ever remain friends with an ex? I don't think I've ever done but there may be plenty of you out there whose bitterness didn't reach quite the volcanic levels mine did.

Friendship After Children

Children too can have a huge effect on friendships; for example, if your best friend doesn't have any kids. The endless fascination that people have with their own children does not automatically rub off on others. Think of your interest in your children and divide by two thousand and there you have your friends' interest in your children.

That is why when you are graphically describing an exploding nappy or Grade One in a clarinet exam, they have slipped into a coma. This points to the fact that you cannot arrange for your group of friends to get pregnant at the same time as you; it's not like synchronising periods you know.

This means that when a woman who has just given birth needs her friends most, they tend to take a back seat. It's a lonely time having a new baby; you are scared and you could do with support. So your best bet is to make friends at NCT (National Childbirth Trust) and then your babies are roughly the same age. I actually didn't want to go to one of these as I was worried about privacy and was justified to some extent when our temporary health visitor went and gossiped about me at a party outside London to a woman who just happened to be my brother's girlfriend. What are the chances of that (to quote Harry Hill)? Ironic that it was a health professional, not someone from an NCT group.

To be honest I probably was a bit lonely and rather envious when I saw groups of women in the park with their babies, but I got through it and enjoyed it apart from the sleepless nights, irritability, rows, panic, to name but a few.

Online information is ubiquitous and you can find anything from medical research to blogs by desperate mums. Despite the number of expensive baby books I ended up with, the thing I found most valuable was a crappy-looking big paperback from our local council for new mothers; it cut through the crap and was as judgement-free as it is possible to be.

Now modern mothers have come into their own, they're all quaffing wine and gin (mother's little helper) like there's no tomorrow in Middleclassland with their friends, whereas I assume there are huge swathes of women soldiering on with the support of the older generation of women in their family who, I would imagine, at that point in their lives turn out to be genuinely their BFFs.

In our day women at home on their own necked Valium; we're all looking for a crutch.

How Has Friendship Changed?

Friendships are very different for teenagers today and for others who are on social media constantly, because it is an absolute minefield of etiquette in terms of how friends behave towards each other. I'm aware of many different situations in which friends don't quite step up to the mark, perhaps because they don't 'like' a photo that you've put up, or they have a party and put it online, and then you realise you weren't invited to it, and you seethe and quietly withdraw your friendship from them. I'd rather be at home not knowing, quite honestly. Social media seems to add a slick layer of cruelty to friendships made and broken. In the olden days ignorance was bliss. Now teenagers and in fact older friends too are forced to face up to the fact they're being crapped on; what a wonderful world. And the power of that little screen to penetrate deep into the centre of those with fragile egos.

No wonder everyone these days is talking about resilience: they bloody need it.

How do young people avoid this pain? Turn off their phones.

Hahahahahahahahahahahah.

How to End a Friendship

There is one theory out there that, in terms of friendship, the whole human race could be split into drains and radiators. Either you are sucking all the life and energy out of things or you are radiating warmth and happiness. I suppose that's another version of the glass-half-full or glass-half-empty person. I think when you need to end a friendship, for most people they have come to the end of their tether having tolerated a lot of bad behaviour for a long time. The moment we feel that a friendship has to end is when those friends of ours are not quite doing it for us, for one reason or another, or indeed, us for them. People whose calls or visits you once looked forward to and now dread. I'm not saying I am potentially the most marvellous friend in the world – I'm certainly not, and I've had friends who have moved away from me. Was I too needy, too bossy or annoying, who knows? But when our friends become too needy or too angry or too whiny, we often decide a certain point has been reached and those friends have to be jettisoned.

That sounds very harsh, doesn't it, but I think most people find it a very difficult thing to do and in some ways it is a tragedy if, like me, you've been on the receiving end of a person trying to 'unfriend' you by simply ignoring you, because they are too embarrassed to tell you the truth about why they don't want to be your friend any more. Obviously social media makes it easy by inventing itself and then inventing ghosting – a way of dumping a partner or finishing a friendship without a whiff of confrontation or unpleasantness; except for the person you've done it to.

I think that is something we could all do with a little instruction in – how to speak honestly to each other – and then we would ultimately end up having better friendships, although the adjustment would be painful at first! Lots of people shy away from discussing unpalatable truths but you can word these conversations so they do not upset the recipient.

If you can face it, just meet the person and speak honestly. If you can't, write them a letter – a proper one on paper, not a bloody email. It's so crap to text someone and dump them or to block them on your social media. If someone's been a good friend at least allow them the dignity of a face-to-face conversation and take the consequences.

If it happens to you, yes it's sad and awful, but why pine over a friend who doesn't like you any more? It's hard to manage emotionally but take the punches and move on. Repeat mantras to yourself like 'What goes around comes around,' and 'Maybe they'll get the Ebola virus,' and search for pastures new. But:

LOWER YOUR EXPECTATIONS!

*

Work very hard on your friendships, because in the long run they are what really count. They anchor you through the stages of your life. Because if you have children, they grow up and leave home. Or you get married, and maybe you stay in that marriage, but it probably changes by its very nature. But a good friend for life, there's nothing like it, so give them a bit of slack if they're annoying because everyone is annoying now and then. Really it's a bit like watering plants: try not to let your friendships wither away because it's hard for them to grow back.

6

HOW TO MANAGE A BULLY

Hecklers are pissed bullies with a loud voice and a big ego. That's why it's so satisfying to nail them – preferably to a wardrobe.

When I was a child at primary school, someone took a boy's shoe bag, swung it round his head several times for maximum impact and hit the boy really hard on the head.

That someone was the headmaster of the school.

And as an eight-year-old, I didn't want similar treatment (although I expect the archaic rules of chivalry would have protected me because I was a girl). However, I kept quiet, as did everyone else in the class, because we were scared shitless.

That is how bullies work.

There are few things that make me angrier than bullying, and perhaps the only thing that makes me angrier than bullying is not being able to run fast enough to catch the bully and hold them down by lying on top of them . . . for a day.

Going to school is normally the first time most of us properly come across bullying. My first experience of children bullying others was a boy in our primary school called Stephen Smith (not his real name) who used to appear to go round randomly hitting people in the playground, until my brother Bill stepped unwittingly into the firing line and became one of his victims.

Bullies tend to have the same attitude as many military leaders, which can be summed up by the phrase, 'You take your punishment like a man and you keep quiet about it.' By the way I am quoting myself there.

Bullies have the sort of radar that enables them to pick on kids who won't fight back on any level; this includes weedy, nerdy, poor, nice, ginger, tall, fat or skinny. Just pick a random adjective as long as it doesn't include the phrase 'fucking massive cage fighter'. My brother Bill was not only quite small as a kid, he was too nice and not possessed of the evil streak bullies recognise in others and then steer clear of.

Looking at the school, in an idyllic setting on the edge of a village green with the church at the top, you could not imagine any badness going on there. Round the back was the inevitable playground, which was L-shaped so there were plenty of opportunities to wreak violence on unsuspecting children.

Stephen Smith picked on my brother a few times. This meant either a slap or some sort of humiliation in front of others, most of whom probably didn't want to laugh, but did so out of fear. I think his tie was nicked and hidden, petty but really bloody irritating.

In the end my brother had had enough and told Stephen Smith that he had joined a boxing club and someone from the club would come down and beat the living daylights out of him if he touched my brother again. Fortunately Stephen Smith was susceptible to this mendacious threat of violence and never risked whacking my brother again.

When I was fifteen I went on a school exchange visit to Germany and stayed with a family in Bonn – not a great success. They took me out for a celebration on Hitler's birthday and tried to make me join in the singsong.

However, when I was out for a moody walk on my own one day, I came across a group of about six children throwing stones at a small boy. As we hadn't covered, 'Please stop stoning that child or I will take you all out with one punch,' in German lessons, I ran at them waving my arms and making weird noises. It had the desired effect; they scattered and I hung around to make sure they didn't come back, asking the boy (roughly seven years old) in halting German if he was okay and not understanding his tearful answer.

The older bullies get, the more of a challenge they are to deal with and have-a-go heroes do not always come off best. If it looks as though it might be dangerous, think hard about whether you are prepared to take the risk. It can be really worth it. I was once with the comic Mark Lamarr in Islington after a show when he spotted a group of about eight young men across the road kicking the crap out of one bloke. Without hesitation Mark ran across the road with me calling him to come back, thinking to myself, He is going to get battered.

Amazingly, he didn't; he got straight into the middle of the fray and talked them out of beating up the little guy, who went one way down the street while the gang went the other. Extraordinary.

As I've already alluded to, the main bullying problems I had at school were actually not from other children, but teachers.

The headmaster's wife was also a bully, but a slightly more subtle one. I once put my hand up twice in the same morning to ask to go to the toilet. She looked at me and said, 'You'll have to bring a potty in tomorrow.' Everyone laughed but I felt extremely humiliated and angry, and lay in bed that night planning her murder.

One of the big issues for me at the time was that the headmaster and his wife were really good friends with my parents, and I could not understand why my parents could not see them for the sadists they were. I didn't say anything at the time, and in fact I don't think I said anything to my mum until I was in my forties or fifties, and she was really, really surprised.

I'm sure most people realise that up to the 1960s and 1970s, and before governments grasped that adults hitting children in the name of education was not acceptable and began to change the rules, teachers could pretty much do what they wanted without any fear of retribution and this included sexual abuse as well.

A friend of my mum's told me that when he was at an all-boys private school, one teacher would walk among the desks apparently about to examine pupils' work and as he bent down to look at the work he would squeeze their crotch and move on. In the jigsaw of sexual abuse this is a tiny piece, but I think it's illustrative of just how common and unremarkable it seemed to the kids. As my mum's friend said, 'We didn't like it, we just put up with it.'

People who are bullies often have a volatile and unpredictable temper and that makes it very difficult being trapped in a room with them. A lot of the time at primary school, there would be a collective intake of breath when Mr or Mrs Basher (his nickname) walked in until we'd sussed out their mood. Given that this was how things were at home quite often, I must have expended a lot of adrenalin during my childhood.

I think everyone knows what bullying is instinctively. It works on two levels: physical and psychological. Bullies torment people in overtly aggressive ways, but also in much more subtle ways too, so that they can actually deny, if challenged, that they are a bully and reframe it as a hilarious joke.

The traditional idea of a bully in my day was the local tough kid off a council estate, who picked on a little ginger kid with glasses who liked reading, and roughed him up a bit. But bullying, as I said, is so much more subtle and varied, imaginative, deniable and soul-crushing than just that.

Amazingly enough there is no real legal definition of bullying. It's something that worms its way into the cracks.

And that is what a bully does. They see an opportunity or a weakness – something that makes someone different – and they pick on it relentlessly. Bullying ranges from people calling you names; either making things up to get you into trouble or taking your friends away from you; hitting, pinching, biting, pushing and shoving; damaging your belongings; stealing your money; posting insulting messages or rumours, in person, on the internet or by IM (cyberbullying); threats and intimidation; making silent or abusive phone calls; to sending you offensive phone texts; bullies can also frighten you so that you don't want to go to school or work, and you pretend to be ill to avoid them.

So What to do About Bullying?

Tell anyone who will listen: friend, teacher, parent, big brother or sister. However, there is a conspiracy of silence surrounding bullying, so you may be too nervous to do that for fear you might be found out. And if you don't feel like you can tell someone in person, write them a note.

Although I am not an advocate of violence I have in the past asked someone big and scary to ask one of my neighbours 'nicely' if he would leave me alone. This individual kept leaving bags of rubbish outside my flat and shouting abuse at me when he got the opportunity. (Maybe he didn't like my jokes.) I'm not sure how 'nicely' my friend asked. Suffice to say I didn't hear a peep out of my neighbour after he'd visited.

I used to fantasise about coming up with the perfect anti-bullying threat. Something like, 'Leave X alone or I'll fucking kill you,' that if it was reported to a parent I could protest that I had been misheard. 'No, I said, "Weave text a bone or I'll chuck in will too."' Yes, that sadly is the best I can do to date – it's a work in progress.

Hissing with Confidence

Pretend you are confident and you don't care. Prepare a couple of put-downs in advance; they don't have to be brilliant, just delivered as if you mean them.

Be aware of how you might come across: James Corden or Mavis from *Coronation Street*? Many of you will have no idea who that second person is. Look her up. I will enjoy the thought of you discovering Mavis. On YouTube. Don't be like her.

When I started as a comedian on the circuit I was very very nervous and because my free hand used to shake so much I used to shove it in the pocket of my very manly suit jacket. This was working very well for me until I saw myself on telly looking like a fat turkey with one wing trying to take off.

However, eventually I got insouciance down to a fine art by managing to stop myself shaking. I would walk on stage looking like I didn't give a toss and if the audience were heckling (dependent on time of night/alcohol consumed) they would usually be shouting abuse. I just used to stand there and stare at them until they got bored and shut up. Either that or I got so drunk I didn't care what they thought of me anyway.

Be a Boy Scout . . . No, Don't Light a Fire. Be Prepared!

Stay in safe areas where the bully can't corner you. Make sure your friends are looking out for you.

Where do Bullies Come From?

I think bullies in many ways are like wasps, aren't they? You can't see any point in them existing. There is no evolutionary reason for them to be quite so horrible.

You will find with lots of bullies, if you dig into their background, that they've had a pretty disturbed child-hood, maybe a violent parent, or an alcoholic parent, perhaps a drug-using parent, and so you might think, Well, it's kind of not their fault. But we have to draw the line somewhere. The problem is, the end result and the damage they do is their fault, so we have to separate out those two issues and treat them in a different way.

I'm afraid letting bullies get away with things because they have had a difficult home life is not the answer. Sure, you can find them help and explore what's going on at home, but you don't want a bully to get the message that their punishment can be negotiated if they introduce extenuating factors.

One thing that is very difficult at school is the huge conspiracy of silence that surrounds bullying. There's something very dishonourable about grassing up a bully, dobbing them in, or whatever phrase you choose to use. In some way it is comparable to adults' whistle-blowing. Now to me, the whole point of whistle-blowing is to reveal some poor care or nursing care going on some-where, and yet the whistle-blower themselves is treated like they are some sort of pariah who's committed a crime, which is an interesting idea when the crime on the whole has been committed by the people that they've reported. Let's hire a PR firm and try and turn the brand around!

A similar thing was said about me when I was swim-ming in the sea and got tired, but it wasn't a PR firm, it was a tug boat.

Mean Girls

To make a massive generalisation, which you may recog-nise by now as my signature dish, many girls seem to have exclusively taught themselves a particularly unpleasant, pernicious kind of verbal bullying. These femmes fatales are rather hilariously called 'the Popular Girls'. This is because they are pretty and this is the envied currency when you are a teenage girl. But for many of the popular girls those lovely looks have produced a bile that is quite breathtaking to behold. If they were just pretty and floated about looking nice, fair enough, but many have taken it upon themselves to judge others from the lofty heights of being beautiful. They are also a good example of what sheep-like, poor judgements teenage girls can make. Still, then they grow up and become very nice.

Pshaw! That is the noise of someone ejaculating sarcas-tically or in disbelief that I think Dickens uses. That may be the most erudite yet unintentionally smutty line I have ever written; and it encapsulates the saying that once a bully always a bully – apart from John Hegley, who has occasionally said he used to be a bully. But I don't believe him.

These popular girls' leader is always, if there was a 'Lady of the Flies', the Jack-ette character. She's more imaginative, she's more emotionally disturbed as well, and you can usually rely on the fact that most of the other popular girls in that group are a little bit frightened of her. They don't seem to realise that if they wanted to they could gang up and push her off her perch. Instead they concentrate their energies on pushing out poor Miss Piggy who has only just worked her way to the outer fringes. (Girls do not like *Lord of the Flies*, and a more balanced book list might be a good idea. Hmm ... might see if any publishers are interested in *Lady of the Flies*.)

The popular girls tend to indulge in humiliation, teasing, verbal abuse about appearance, tricks, niggling acts like constantly poking someone in the back with a pencil during a lesson, taking the piss about someone's appearance on Instagram posts and the like, stealing things, hiding things, and they're kind of like superannuated nuns gone bad on Xanax. The popular girls tend to be from better-off families, spoiled and, shall we say, not so academic? However in some schools bright people or sporty people are the popular ones and less likely to be bullies.

We had some popular girls in our school, two years above us, who were very pretty, looked down on everyone and every lunch hour would practise their Pan's People (off to

YouTube with you) dance in the school hall to the hit song of the time, George Harrison's 'My Sweet Lord'. My little nerdy-comes-in-all-shapes-and-sizes friend group used to stand at the back taking the piss. It was very childish, but, God, was it fun.

However when it comes to adults, teachers who bully already have an advantage because of their size. They can't use the cane any more, but they can shout, humiliate, talk down to, over-punish and pick on individuals.

How we deal with bullying is interesting: lots of charities have set up helplines so that kids can call them and say how awful they feel, but to me this doesn't get to the nub of actually sorting out the bullies. It's all very well for us to go, 'Oh, isn't life terrible and aren't bullies horrible,' but that just means the bullies are still bullying, and the people who've been bullied are a little bit more emotionally damaged than they were. So we do need to come up with something slightly more effective, in my opinion.

I think schools should have a dedicated website on which pupils can write tales of bullying they have experienced. This could be run by volunteer older pupils who are perhaps a bit more savvy about what actually goes on. Bullying could be categorised into levels of violence – verbal and physical – in a points system and pupils who get over ten points, say, in a month, have to be seen by the bullying group and the accusations investigated. Given that reporting bullying is something most pupils don't want to do, some incentive has to be given. Perhaps you could think up how that would work, dear reader?

My major advice would be TAKE IT SERIOUSLY. The most frustrating thing about bullies is they always get away with it.

If you want to help someone who is being bullied I'd recommend the online anti-bullying sites [see page 289]. Cop-out, yes, but why regurgitate when I can redirect?

Managing a Bully in Life

In stand-up there are endless opportunities for audience members to bully the act on stage but, it must be said, it is two-way traffic and many comics relish getting stuck into a hapless pissed punter in the front row who's had, quite frankly, a pathetic go at the act and then realises he's made a big mistake as his personality is dismantled bit by bit in front of an audience of similarly pissed people.

However, let's concentrate on traffic going the other way. It's important for comics, especially female comics who still tend to get picked on more about their appearance than men, to have a few heckle put-downs up their sleeve and a plan about what to do if things get out of hand. There are several types of punters who heckle.

1. Mr So Pissed He Just Makes Weird Groaning Noises: get him removed.
2. Mr Watch This, Lads, I'll Sort This Uppity Bird Out: be like a teacher and alienate him from his friends and make them laugh at him.

3. Mr Scary May Have Just Come out of Prison for Some Sort of Sexual Misconduct: have your most horrible put-down ready or call security.

4. Mr I Think You'll Find I'm Funnier Than You, Love: kill him! (With your words.)

5. Mr Does Actually Say Something Really Witty and This Floors You: acknowledge his brilliance and move on. No point trying to fight a brilliant line.

Obviously I've been practising put-downs for years and I'm still scared someone will beat me, but pretending I don't care is my favourite armour.

Gird your loins and get out there!

7

HOW NOT TO FALL IN LOVE (AND OTHER ADVICE YOU'LL IGNORE)

I can hold my breath under water for about a minute. My husband can do much longer – with a little help from me.

When you are a teenager your feelings are magnified to the point of almost suffocating you and they are amplified by selecting and playing tortured songs as the theme tune to your pain – in my case, Bob Dylan, Neil Young and everyone's favourite self-debasing lord of sex and obsession, Leonard Cohen. Add to that some appalling poetry penned by your own hand (you're in luck, I destroyed it all), and a sense of your family as Capulets and his as Montagues, even though in reality with my forbidden romance our parents never met and, although they almost certainly would have intensely disliked each other, it's highly unlikely his dad would have attempted to run mine through with his sword. And you do all those clichéd things that millions of people have done for years before you, while still believing you are unique. Each millisecond is exquisite torture as you wait for the phone to ring, obsessively observing every minuscule change in their tone of voice just in case they've gone off you ... it is completely unbearable, the whole bloody thing.

And it's just as unbearable and ridiculous to the people who are forced to live with you, although a damned sight more entertaining for them.

The idea that I would even have a boyfriend before I was fifty-five was a bit of a freakish idea to my parents, so when a long-haired, posh, arrogant, drug-using, boozy, ex- public schoolboy hove into view my dad's hackles rose so high that they fired his paternal and socialist zeal to levels hitherto unreached.

We'd met because he kept coming into Boots the Chemist where I worked on Saturdays and his arrival each week was more eagerly anticipated by me than tea break. Looking back, I am aware that he was an entitled (and lovable at times) arse, as every single friend I had warned me off him, even the ones who had never met him who were just going by reputation. He weighed two stone, could down fifteen pints a night and was a dedicated drug-user: every mother's dream.

I had kept his existence a secret from my mum and dad because I knew what they would think. My friends received every utterance about him as if I were the first Mrs Rochester and smiled indulgently through:

'I hate him, the bastard.'
'I can't live without him.'

'Can you come to his house with me?'

'Do you think his phone's broken?'

'Do you know anyone who would kill him for me?'

When I brought him home to meet my parents my dad lamped him because he thought he was taking the piss when in fact he genuinely was that stupidly posh and theatrical. Yes, he was a wanker, but he was a wanker I had the misfortune to be in love with.

Home life consisted of shouting matches punctuated by short periods of relative peace. As arguments got longer and peace got shorter, my mum and dad, under duress and because they obviously couldn't stand it any longer, said unless I ditched him I had to move out. I went joyfully to a slightly crappy bedsit and never looked back once.

I got a tedious job in the civil service, and went back to school once a week. He met me at weekends, always in the same pub on Friday nights, except one night I got there early to catch him in flagrante with another woman and lost it completely. The dream was over. I think that was probably the beginning, as Lady Gaga would have put it, of learning that it's a very good idea to be able to put on a p-p-p-p-p-p-p-poker face. I pretended things were fine nonetheless and that gave me lots of options because he genuinely believed I wasn't bothered.

So I made a radical decision and I left. I hired a van, packed all my stuff into it and moved out of the bedsit, leaving the few things that belonged to him and no forwarding address. It was one of the toughest decisions I've ever made. I had to rescue myself from myself and after that I became a very mature, considerate and well-balanced person. That's if you consider a sixteen-year-old revenge-seeking, drunken adolescent mature.

Can I start by saying that I think passionate is one of the most misused words in the English language. I've even heard someone saying, 'I'm passionate about insoles.' How can you be passionate about something as banal as insoles? Every time you turn on the TV and see someone talking about charity, or their career, they are either passionate about it or they're on a journey, both of which make me want to retch and reach into the TV and shake them hard.

Falling in love has been compared to mental illness, the type that is called psychosis, which means being out of touch with reality. It is certainly very hard to read about other people falling in love, because I'm not sure anyone else's experience can ever really match your own, or describe it in the words that you would use.

The rather prosaic fact that I remember about the science of falling in love is that there are identifiable stages. There's the first stage, where you are completely bonkers and all you can think about is them. You get butterflies in your stomach, la la la la, all the rest of it. But then, several weeks down the line, more pragmatic concerns start to enter your life, and you start thinking, How could this ever work out, when I'm a fan of Jeremy Corbyn and they are the leader of UKIP. (By the way, just in case you are thinking, Is that true? No, it's what we call a joke . . . ish.)

Then there are all those rather tedious practical factors: political beliefs, the way in which people live their lives, does your partner have a dog that you can't stand? All these have to be worked through before you decide if you're going to progress down the line.

The Italians, who are supposed to be the most passionate race, certainly in Europe, did some research a few years ago and said that the sort of romantic love that results in you being completely at one with your beau and you can't think of anything else doesn't last that long. At the very outside, it lasts two years, which is slightly depressing in many ways, isn't it? Clearly you do get the very rare couple who are still holding hands and gazing into each other's eyes when they are well into their eighties, but I can't say that I've ever met any of them. Good luck to them, but I don't think it happens very often.

The Sexism of Sexual Attraction

I'm sure you are aware of the concept of punching above your weight. For instance, if a very attractive young woman dates a rather old, grumpy bloke, we will say he is punching above his weight. In the case of men as potential partners, their wealth, their fame, their sense of humour – all these things come to bear on whether women can overlook shortcomings in their physical appearance. To some extent, it does work in reverse as well, but it is far more likely that you will see elderly, wealthy men paired with young and beautiful women than the other way round. So men who service younger women are sugar daddies whereas women who are 'being serviced' shall we say, even though it makes them sound like washing machines, tend to be known as cougars, i.e. prowlers. If there was ever a worse misnomer that actually applied to men, answers on a postcard please. Younger male partners are always called 'toyboys', which I now realise is in the sense of a cougar toying with the lifeless body of its prey rather than pushing buttons or hanging buckets on his protuberances.

Is there such a thing as falling in love at first sight? Again, that's very difficult to say. I think you might look at someone across a room and think, Cor, they're quite nice! (sorry, went a bit Ealing Comedy there) and then spend the rest of your life with them, but I shouldn't think that occurs very often. It's certainly never happened to me.

But maybe love at first sight is more something that happens to very attractive people. I was thinking the other day about falling in love at first sight – does that work if you are unattractive, or even ugly? I have a feeling that all this stuff about love does tend to revolve around being attractive. Poetry is about attractive people, so is art, and novels are too, on the whole. Mr Rochester in *Jane Eyre* is supposed to be pug ugly but in films he is always portrayed by a handsome film-star type (everyone from Orson Welles to Michael Fassbender) with a bit of five o'clock shadow to signify he's in a bit of a state.

So those of us who are trailing quite a long way behind the attractive people, who don't really have the benefit of good looks, or indeed what is considered an acceptably lovely body, have to do the very best we can. I believe that what is ignored by art, journalism and novels is the way that people who aren't very attractive just get on with their lives and have the same feelings as beautiful people. You're probably thinking, Well, that's absolutely bloody obvious, and it is in some ways, but if it is so obvious, why don't we see more films and more plays with an entire cast of ugly people in them? If you do see any, they tend to be freak shows, which are put together for our entertainment.

Imagine, respected reader, if you could come up with a list of films with not very attractive people in them . . . I'll start you off with *Shrek*. You get no points for anything with me in it. I've already pre-empted that potential heckle!

One upside of not being gorgeous is that if you aren't the beautiful princess waiting patiently to be rescued by a handsome prince, and becoming excessively dull while you do, because you don't actually have to make an effort to be interesting, well-informed, educated and amusing, then you can do what you bloody well want as you go along and choose the right one for you – within the bounds of reason obviously – hopefully without kissing too many frogs along the way. Although I've heard they're brilliant kissers.

Breaking the Ice

In the olden days, it was generally accepted that men would approach women and stake a claim with them, running the risk of being rejected and made to look foolish. However that was not quite as bad as sitting there night after night in the dark, sadly waiting for someone/anyone to come and chat to you, wondering whether you'll have to include other mammals in your list of acceptable partners. Chatting people up or its modern equivalent is risky but recently women have also taken the initiative and run the risk of rejection more. I fear there is no such thing as putting out risk-free feelers to potential partners so maybe construct a chat-up line that gives you a get-out clause if you don't get anywhere.

I think if you went up to them and said something like, 'You look really nice and I'd like to buy you a drink,' and they turn you down, then follow it up with, 'Well, looks can be deceiving, you are actually a twat. Could I suggest a tattoo just to warn people?'

Or maybe disguise your motive until you know if they're going for it. So . . .

You: 'Hi, Ellie Wilson sends her love.'

He: 'Who's Ellie Wilson?'

You: 'Me.'

If he's not bowled over by your cleverness: 'Actually, I'm not Ellie Wilson but she is just the type of person who would like you – a very poor judge of character.'

I think the idea of hideous punny chat-up lines has been gestated for far too long by shows like *Blind Date*. Avoid anything that has the whiff of sleaze, a pun or a phallic or vaginal symbol in it.

How Compos Mentis Do You Need to be to Properly Chat Someone Up?

Most people, when they're on their way to potentially meet a future partner, be it at a club or a pub or even a blind date, sometimes need a little help to calm their nerves. Admittedly a drink can sort out social anxiety but it's all a question of balance.

It depends whether it's that time of night when you're fresh out of the shower, smelling lovely and your face is immaculate or the desperate time of the night when even a Tory will do, your face has moved down on to your neck, make-up-wise, and you are nearly on your knees begging anyone that goes past to notice you.

One thing to remember is that although alcohol oils the wheels of wit and small talk, tip over the edge and you are rambling a bit and being as boring as the Scottish football results to a Welsh person, so be careful how much you have.

Ditto cigarettes: they do soothe the butterflies thing but they don't leave a particularly attractive aroma lingering round your mouth. If you're trying to pull a non-smoker you probably need to have the looks of someone like Cara Delevingne to get beyond first base. So, the odd fag to calm your nerves followed by an industrial-forest-denuding spray of mouth freshener might do the trick.

If you realise you are talking gibberish, then rather than clumsily depart from the situation make a feature of this. You could say something like, 'Sorry if I'm talking crap, I'm always like this when I've just had my travel inoculations.'

This has a twofold effect: it makes you sound interesting;[*] and also, if he is a penetrate-and-piss-off kind of guy you'll give yourself a chance to decide if you want to go for a no-strings night because he'll be thinking, At least she's leaving soon so I won't have to hide from her if she likes me too much.

How to Spot a Wrong 'Un

Another thing to bear in mind about love is that damaged people aren't very good at it, and those who are damaged by their family dynamics very early on in their lives don't have a sign round their neck saying that is the case. This happens much more these days, where online dating is all about looks; many people pick someone who looks gorgeous and then find they are a complete emotional mess that they want to run away from.

They have to find that out for themselves, although we could have some sort of system, like a little box up in the corner of Tinder, saying, 'smashed up the house twice, kicked my dog' or 'put cheese in my shoes', giving all those lovely faces a suitability rating. Someone I know met an Arab guy at a club and spent the night in his hotel with him. When she woke up in the morning he had gone but there was £3,000 on the pillow; he'd taken her for a high-class prostitute. NB: This is just a story, I'm not suggesting you make this part of your dating ambitions.

---

[*] Maybe government work in the Galapagos Islands.

Stalking

So how do men and women differ when they are madly in love with someone, but they can't have them?

Stalking has become a major problem for both sexes, although people tend to think it is worse if it is a man doing it, because on the whole men have more physical strength, more testosterone coursing around, so they are more likely to lose their temper and be threatening and violent. This presupposes that men being stalked by a woman can sort it out by threatening physical violence, but of course not all men are like this.

Being stalked is a terrifying and nightmarish experience for whomever is at the receiving end and demonstrates the huge numbers of disturbed people who seem to be able to move around terrifying the life out of others.

One huge problem with stalking, as if the stalking itself isn't bad enough, is the way in which it is dealt with by the police. No one is naïve enough to assume the police can supply round-the-clock protection for everyone, in which case, if you think the problem is serious, you need to do something yourself. I'm not going to make any suggestions here, but there are many websites to help you with safety ideas. This is particularly difficult if an ex-partner is stalking you and you have children together. Recently the law has been changed to try and protect people further from stalkers. It seems women are three to five times more likely to be stalked than men.

My feeling is we should push for more protection for men who are being stalked, since, in a cynical way, I believe something may then change. This is because woven into the fabric of our society is the message that men are more important than women.

The Physical Side of Romance

Once you have met someone that you like and you really fancy, and navigated all the initial minefields, should you leap into bed? Well, traditionally, sleeping with them on the first date was fine if you were a bloke and not fine if you were a woman. But times are changing and the tables turning and I have noticed that my teenage daughters now have a word for a bloke who sleeps around. He's called a fuckboy. That's a very descriptive phrase, isn't it? It's the same present in a different package if you like, because lots of men have always kept their options open. If you don't want to be an option that's being kept open, you need to try and be tough. Most women have a sense of that happening, but lots allow themselves to ignore it. Don't ignore it or you'll end up like the poor seventy-three women juggled by Adam on *Love Island*. (At the time of writing it's only three but I am expecting the number to rise massively by the end of the series). I don't know if things have changed that much and women still tend to get the vast majority of stern gazes directed towards them if they have a lot of sexual partners.

A phrase I really hate is when people say, 'I'm in lust.' No, you're not. You just don't particularly like the person. You don't love them, you simply want to have sex with them. I know that's a long way round to them saying 'I'm in lust,' but if you are someone who uses that word – can you stop doing it.

What Do You/They Really Want?

Something that is very common in the frustrating dance of lurve is game playing (no, not Scrabble, Doris), because men and women do conduct relationships very differently from one another. Women often feel they have to play one, called the 'Pretend I Don't Care About Him' game, because if you do admit your feelings in a rush of passion to someone, apparently it scares the crap out of them and nine times out of ten they do one down the road.

A lot of men like to control the progress of a relationship so if they start early with their evil male manipulation, that sets them up further down the line to call the shots. I think it's a confidence thing. It's a with-holding thing. Lots of women can't understand why when they've had a brilliant night with a guy, he doesn't want to text them back forty-seven seconds later.

I would say to young women, think seriously about what it is you want in a relationship. I've noticed a lot of women, and I include myself in the early days as well, if someone doesn't call, they will ring them desperately on speed dial until the object of their affections tells them to go away or calls the police. It is quite hard for women not to have the exact future circumstances of their relation-ship mapped out for them in the first week. Yes, I may be generalising here but a straw poll of my experiences tells me this is true. Women want to know. Women can't help that and men play on it. I would suggest to women who always get themselves into this love pickle in every relationship that they actually practise some self-restraint and almost train themselves not to flirt and prematurely blurt ... It's so easy to do. (That's another whole can of worms: when to do the ILY thing. I once thought someone had said it to me and said it back to them only to be met with a look of confusion and horror – that one didn't go very far!)

You could try, if someone asks you out, saying you're busy, not answering their texts for a day, counting three calls from them before you phone back or leaving a date early and mysteriously; but you've got to follow through or it's a waste of time. C'mon, give 'em a taste of their own You're-Not-That-Important-To-Me medicine.

The sexes can often have different interpretations of fidelity. Women are very strongly discouraged from straying – an adulterous wife runs the risk of being stoned to death in some cultures – while for men it is considered to be a bit exciting and makes them rather dashing and attractive. I include in this all kinds of men in the public eye, who unashamedly dump a wife once she has got to a certain age. I can understand if you've been in a long-term relationship, you are fed up with your partner, you find their habits very annoying and everything they say irritates you – but suddenly to be seen out and about a week later with someone very like them, except a lot younger, says something really disappointing about the human race and about men in particular.

What Happens If Your Friends Hate Them – Or They Hate Your Friends?

One other issue that can be quite a problem in relationships is what happens if your friends think your partner's a knob. That's very difficult indeed and you have to keep them apart, or persuade both sides to have a bit of respect for each other, or you will have to drop either your friends or your partner. All of which are very tough decisions to make.

I have had several relationships with people my friends couldn't stand, mainly because the man in question made me so unhappy by pissing about and being unreliable, and at those times I didn't take the advice I have given you, but wish I had. Low self-esteem is a major component of taking a lot of crap and if it's a pattern in your life you might want to consider getting some help. There is loads everywhere. To some extent for me it was like being an alcoholic and I couldn't bring myself to do anything about it despite what my friends said until I absolutely hit rock bottom, and I learned from that. It's the situation in which a woman drops all her friends one by one that alarm bells need to be rung. On the other hand, if your friend has a boyfriend who you can't stand who is not mistreating her in any way and she seems really keen on him, hold your tongue for as long as you can unless you feel really justified about some piece of unacceptable behaviour.

Don't Forget Your Friends

I know I'm repeating myself here but – this is vitally important – if you are going to have a relationship with someone, however mad you are about them, please make an effort to hang on to your friends. I have seen it happen so many times: when someone in a friendship group or that I know pretty well meets a new person, and they disappear off the radar for six months, a year, five years, even ten years, and then you get a call in the middle of the night. They want to go back to how things were, because they need you to pick up the pieces after he has run off with the violin teacher next door. It's rather insulting when this happens and if you haven't made a real effort to keep up your friendships, then you can't expect anyone to come running when your relationship goes wrong.

How to Survive Being Dumped

The most painful thing that can happen to you if you are in love is to be rejected by the person you love. There's only one bit of advice I can give here and you don't have to listen to it, because who am I to give you advice? (And as I said, I can't deny that, in similar situations, I've ignored enormous amounts of well-meant advice.) But I would say if someone says they don't want to be with you, YOU HAVE TO BELIEVE THAT. You must not think they don't mean it, they love me really, or they're only testing me to see whether I love them, or they're playing a game with me. BELIEVE IT ... AND GET

OUT OF THERE! Your box of tissues won't be intact but your self-esteem will be.

We have to take these sorts of things seriously and if someone says they're going to ring you and they don't, that means they don't want to see you or they want to control the relationship and see you when they want to. Either way they're a twat. This is all from bitter experience. (Once, after I hadn't been away from home for very long I had a brief relationship with someone who said they really liked me but didn't want us to be seen out together so we could only meet at my home and I put up with that for far longer than I should have done and kept it quiet from my friends because I knew exactly what they would say.)

I'm sorry to be harsh. I think we all have to learn our own way of dealing with rejection. It's impossible in many ways, because it makes you feel like such a piece of shit when someone turns you down and suddenly your world has got a big, dark blanket thrown over it and you don't know what to do. People will be desperate to help but just don't know what to say, so they flail about throwing clichés at you.

Time is a great healer.
Plenty more fish in the sea.
Always thought you'd be the one leaving him.
Never liked him anyway.
His clothes were really embarrassing.
You were too good for him.
He is an arsehole.
He's got a conviction for murder (all right, not that one then).

None of the advice, like go and join an evening class or knit your own shroud or whatever, is particularly helpful and we need to find a way around all that sort of stuff. If you take away one thing from this, please let it be that you delete all social media contact with your ex and bar their number (and then avoid all social media). Pretend they died.

They should be dead to you now anyway, but don't go as far as being the one who tries to make them dead.

8

HOW TO DO WHAT YOU WANT (AND NOT WHAT OTHERS WANT YOU TO DO)

I've started ordering my own birthday cake with the words I want on it. Ordered one recently that said, 'You are a very old woman'. When I picked it up I opened the box and it said, 'Happy Retirement, Wendy'. Whoops, hope Wendy's not too pissed off with hers.

I am one person who did get to do what I wanted. From around eleven or twelve, the idea was starting to form in my head that I might be able to make people laugh, as a job. It took a long time to come to anything, because I was too scared of looking like a fool, of being crap and it not working out. It took me till I was twenty-nine – which I think is fairly late – to decide to have a bash at it as a career. By which point I'd tried all kinds of other jobs.

I'd pulled the heads off chrysanthemums in a nursery, the tedium of which could only be matched by an extended programme on the budget, worked at Boots, where I gave unasked-for advice on make-up about which I knew nothing, and in a Victorian residential home for adults with learning disabilities, the head of which made Mr Squeers looks like a wet liberal.

So, after I'd finished university and worked full time as a nurse for several years, a night out in the pub with friends finally pointed me in the direction of comedy. I had bored the arses off my friends by whining on endlessly about wanting to do stand-up. One friend of mine said to me, 'Oh for God's sake stop moaning on about it. Either do it or shut up about it.'

So I did. I agreed to do a benefit gig in Soho for a friend and somehow, displaying extreme naïvety and ignorance, thought I would be fine going on at midnight after all the booked comedy acts.

Everything was wrong about the night. The gig was at a club in Soho that had probably never been used for comedy before, the audience were obviously not very comedy literate, by which I mean used to the rhythm of a comedy show, and quite a lot of them were quite drunk. In contrast *I* was *extremely* drunk. I waited four hours to go on, consuming lager like . . . well, lager . . . and so when the compere announced my name I staggered on and began to parrot my hilarious material about Sigmund Freud. I'd probably had about seven pints of lager.

What I hadn't really factored in was that every professional act on the bill, including one of my all-time favourites Johnny Immaterial, had pretty much died on their arse, so how on earth I imagined I could do any better I don't know. That is the wonderful ego-insulating power of alcohol; at least one person in the room thought I was hilarious – and that person was me.

As soon as words came out of my mouth, someone started to heckle from the back, and that person was a maverick comic, who, along with his mate, did avant-garde stuff on stage like rolling on broken glass or setting fire to his trousers.

Rather than just the one heckle, one or both of these characters, I can't really remember, started to chant, 'Fuck off, you fat cow,' continuously until I did in fact fuck off, probably after about three minutes. Couldn't really remember much after that.

This was in August 1986 and I suppose a lot of people would have given up at this point, but it gradually dawned on me that doing a benefit show in which no one is really invested might not be the best way to start.

So I left it three months, wrote some new material and booked myself into a proper comedy club in New Cross for a five-minute guest spot. This went much better, and someone watching in the audience booked me for a proper show with proper money at the Gate Theatre in Notting Hill. That went well apart from the fact that when I heard the compere announce my name I realised I had no idea how to get on to the stage – and ended up in desperation crawling out from under the curtain at the back of the stage. This got a big laugh and rather than being embarrassed I decided to pretend I'd done it deliberately. The same went for being unable to get the microphone off the stand and breaking that. Another big laugh and I was on my way. I thought, Now it's all going to be plain sailing.

Wrong.

I did a lot of really, really shit gigs, where people hated me, and I got knocked back a lot, and then finally it all started to come together. I suppose it was when I was invited to perform at the Comedy Store in London, rather than having to beg them for a slot, that I realised I could sort of do comedy.

If you have an ambition, then you owe it to yourself to have a crack at it. Just be sensible in setting your goals. If you love nature, hate teenagers and wake up early every morning, then maybe you could achieve that dream of becoming a park-keeper. If you want to be a ballet dancer and you weigh forty-three stone, well, then you need to lose thirty-five stone. But if you want to be a pop star and are fifty-seven with a voice like Rod Stewart's mum having an unanaesthetised hysterectomy, then possibly you should think again about your options.

But the first hurdle you are going to encounter if you want to be an astronaut, or a professor of geography, or whatever it may be, is education. I know I sound like somebody's mum (well, I am somebody's mum), but the people who end up struggling the most in life are generally the ones who pissed about at school. It is hard when you are a teenager to be told, 'If you do nothing at school then you won't get a decent job.' But unfortunately that is the case, nine times out of ten. You may be thinking, yes, but what about all these people who got no GCSEs and went on to run huge businesses. They are very much the exception. Katie Price, for example, is always held up as someone from a very modest background who survived the world of glamour modelling and now runs her own business, even though recently things have gone a bit wrong for her, but that doesn't mean that hundreds of thousands of teenage girls who would like to do that will have the same success.

When I was growing up, people's ambitions were reasonably modest, and I am talking about kids here, saying, 'I want to be a fireman,' or 'I want to be a nurse,' and those sorts of ambitions are genuinely achievable. I can't really remember what I wanted to be as an eight-year-old but as I was beyond desperate to own a pony, it was probably something to do with that. (The pony-owning thing never happened by the way as we were not that sort of family.)

These days, teenagers are bombarded by images across social media of their heroes, who have built up followings of millions by sitting in their bedrooms doing make-up demonstrations, or tying up their cat and squirting it with tomato ketchup. They are precocious, they have got no sense whatsoever of anyone else's existence in the world apart from their own: they are just capitalist monsters, selling every aspect of their lives to other teenagers who can ill afford it.* And the worst thing is that they have become role models.

* Having said that, the democracy of the internet is a great thing: I would so much rather a singer became famous because lots of people liked their song on YouTube, than some bland boy-child relentlessly plugged by a record company.

Is this a bit harsh? Yes, of course it is. I have overlaid my own uncompromising and almost universally unpopular opinion re commercial activity over the top of teenagers who think it is perfectly normal to promote products and don't see anything wrong with it. I'm prepared to accept I am a bit of a twanny about these things, although the YouTuber who went to a suicide forest and took the piss with some poor bastard hanging from a tree in the background had totally lost the plot. I have watched a few episodes of *Keeping Up with the Kardashians* with my daughters, one of whom is not that keen. I furiously list the shameless product placement going on in the episode while they, of course, especially the one who likes it, soak up the exciting (?) life of a family hell-bent on promoting themselves whatever the cost.

Those who are part of the intelligentsia consider themselves to be above shows like *Keeping Up with the Kardashians*, which they find distasteful. Shameless flaunting of wealth, blatant product placement and promotion of their own businesses. Yes, these things are horribly immoral and unpalatable, but above all *KUWTK* is BORING and I hope that does for them in the end.

But it has to be said that the Kardashians have more followers than there are people on the planet and so their 'look' is popping up all over the shop. I am waiting till the day that our lollipop lady has plumped up her booty and got enormous pointy bosoms before I finally cave in and accept they rule the world.

I suppose the obsession with being famous is not quite as far from reality as it was when I were a young'un. Lots of *young people* . . . God I hate that phrase so I'm going to call them *adolescent humans* because 'young people' is what politicians call them and what the fuck do they know?

Sorry, got diverted . . . Lots of adolescent humans are internet- and camera-savvy and many of them speak to it as if they've been presenting *News at Ten* for donkey's years. So it's not such a leap to think someone could be plucked from obscurity to be a presenter . . . just not two million of them.

As children become teenagers and then adults, their early ambitions often fall by the wayside. They can be distracted by problems, whether it is issues with their parents, difficulties at school, mental health issues, maybe trouble with boyfriends or girlfriends. It is so easy not to be single-minded about what we want to do. There is something that is quite impressive, I suppose, about the upper middle classes who absolutely drive their children into the ground, trying to get them to do what they want. That is how we end up with a parliament full of mainly middle-class people, who are utterly searing in their attempt to arrive at where they want to be. The aristocracy just expect it to happen. It would be great if people from different backgrounds were able to apply the same single-minded ambition to their lives, without the help of their parents, because if we are honest, a lot of working-class parents are simply too busy working hundreds of hours to make ends meet to have the time to encourage their kids to move up a notch.

There are simple things you can do to walk towards your chosen career. First of all, you have to find out as much information as possible about what you need to do.

As far as comedy was concerned, when I was younger I thought being an actor would be good enough, but as 'alternative comedy' took hold, I realised that it would take more than being able to trot out 'The quality of mercy' speech. I looked through comedy listings, read articles and tried to work out which comedy clubs would go a bit easy on me (vegetarian restaurant in Archway and a tiny little club above a pub near Tottenham Court Road). And which wouldn't (Jongleurs in Battersea, stag nights a-go-go, and the Tunnel in Greenwich – totally randomly aggressive audience, on occasion missiles thrown at the acts). Most of what you learn about comedy is learned once you start but that's not the same for everything.

I remember one of the mums I know telling me that she helped out at an academy interviewing pupils to give them some advice about how to approach universities.

One girl she spoke to said she was really keen to do economics at university so she asked her to describe a recent story in the news that was of interest to her and related to economics. Cue very long silence. This is exactly the sort of thing that will NOT impress potential employers or universities; at the very least spend half an hour thinking of something to say about the area you want to work in instead of some banal crap like, 'Oh I really like it,' which will make the interviewer slip into a coma. The other thing I would say is USE A SPELLCHECKER. Lots of potential employees will frown upon the fact not that you can't spell but that you couldn't be bothered to get it right.

And try to appear confident, which helps enormously, but you do have to have something to back it up with or you will be found out on the job. Anyone who has sexed up their CV needs to be careful.

However, had social media been around when I was an adolescent human, I'd never have got any job, consisting as my teenage years did of behaving very badly.

You have to track down the people who might be helpful; you need to pester them with letters or emails about your ambition, and you must not be put off by being let down. Women, in particular, do tend to lack confidence and not being put off by waves of rejection is a huge element in moving towards what you really want to do.

I have been rejected more times than I've had hot dinners and you can tell how many hot dinners I've had just by looking at me.

I once went for a role in a prison drama playing an ex-beauty queen (all right, that last bit isn't true). The role was a very dangerous psychopath (this was the nineties) and as I squirmed uncomfortably in front of five or so of the least sympathetic people in the world, I could tell I wasn't going to get it so I started to piss about and tease them with the medical language of psychiatry that they couldn't possibly have known. Suffice to say I didn't land the job and I dealt with it by recasting the panel as the problem.

In the world of comedy, for comedy jobs I had a couple of very supportive friends who would come to shows with me and take me straight off to a pub if it had gone badly.

When I first got on stage as a comic, I was absolutely terrified, but the thing is that you can act confident. I have often pretended to be far more confident than I am and usually that's enough. I used to stare blankly at the audience as if I couldn't give a shit, and for some reason that worked. My stage name was 'the Sea Monster'. I built up a reputation that I didn't really care what people thought of me, and that I actively liked taking on hecklers shouting revolting abuse. None of that was true. I didn't like it at all, but the fact that I appeared to be okay with it got me through my early career.

I think as human beings, we are the ones who know ourselves the best, so you will instinctively be aware if you cannot genuinely get through something that terrifies you or if you can at least have a go. For example, I couldn't walk along Striding Edge in the Lake District without panicking, slipping over and sliding down it on my bum, so I will never try that because it is quite high. On the other hand, I possibly could have a go at swimming the Channel, although I must stress that will NEVER HAPPEN because it's not on my bleeding bucket list. When I was a baby comic and things didn't immediately go well, I kept going by setting myself a limit on the time that I would continue to flog a dead horse if necessary. There's nothing better than writing a joke that absolutely smashes it the first time you perform it, but this very seldom happens. However, there is pleasure in working on a joke and trying to get it right each time you do a show. My favourite kind of laugh is one that keeps rolling, dies down slightly during the next joke and then builds again, rolling like a wave through your set. This is pretty rare but when it happens it's such a lovely moment.

I never had any problems at all in multiple dressing rooms across the country. I felt at home, fitted in with people and made good friends, which made me realise that these were people I could get on with and I should drop any ideas I had of becoming madam of a brothel. People tended to be supportive, rowdy horrible gigs were approached as if we were all in it together and the compere was sent out into the fray to report back on the conditions: 'They're really pissed, don't do your routine about knitting elves and watch the stag party on the right-hand side, the ringleader's called Shane.'

I think a lot of comedians feel like outsiders and many go through their careers still feeling like this. It is a bit of a solitary pastime being a stand-up but if you want to you can go down a route that offers you more of a communal experience like being in a play or doing improvisation.

The other thing about confidence is that if you act confident and resilient for long enough, it does start to seep into your bones. And then suddenly, there you are feeling like you could conquer the world.

YOUR CHOICE IS THE RIGHT CHOICE

To me, feminism is about choice, so if you want to stay at home and have loads of kids and that is your ambition, then do it. Don't feel bad about it, or let people put pressure on you. On the other hand, if you don't want to have kids, and want to have an amazing career and travel the world, do that. People are so judgemental about women without children and I don't understand that at all. Bollocks to them.

The other thing we all want is to be happy. The problem with this is that most people don't realise they are happy until they are unhappy, and they look back regretfully and say, 'Oh, I was really happy then and it has all gone wrong now. Why didn't I appreciate it at the time?' It is similar to not appreciating good health, I suppose. As soon as you get ill, you are appalled by how cavalier you were with your health. That is down to people finding it difficult to picture being ill. When you haven't got a headache, you can't imagine what one feels like, even though you know it is awful.

We have to be realistic about what happiness is. And when we are, we'll be a lot happier. To a lot of people, making it means living in a bloody great mansion, having a butler, owning loads of clothes, driving a big car and all the rest of it. But I can tell you, I have met loads of people who have got that sort of thing who are no happier than you or I. People always argue that it is much easier to be happy in a big mansion with a butler and a big fuck-off car. (The old being-miserable-in-comfort argument.) Yes, that is true, but it is also easy to be happy if life is less complicated and you don't have very much at all. We all need to work on how to make ourselves feel happy and how not to let other people bring us down. We have to tell those people to go away and stop being so bad-tempered and annoying us.

In the olden days women's ambitions were pretty limited, but these days theoretically women can do what they want. Let's face it, women in male-dominated professions do get a bit of stick but if you really want to do it you will find a way. There are still many women stuck in a netherworld of low pay and uncertain futures.

I always thought Princess Diana was a very good example of a real person who, from the outside, looked like she had achieved everything she could have possibly wanted, as far as tradition dictates for women anyway (and this has happened again with Meghan Markle). Diana had married a rich prince in a fairy-tale wedding, her life was glamorous and she was beautiful, ticking all the boxes on the traditional female happy-ending checklist. I met her once and I thought she was utterly charming, and I'm a republican. She had a wicked sense of humour and was very funny, and I feel sad that her life ended so early and that she probably was not happy for much of her time as an adult.

While we are on the whole concept of doing what you want and getting what you want, can we chat briefly about the idea of bucket lists, which I have always found very annoying. The thing about bucket lists is that they feel like clichéd arrows, pointing towards something that is brilliant and will make you happy. I might be a weirdo, but I don't really think seeing the Pyramids of Giza is going to do very much for me, because I don't like the heat and I have seen a picture of them and they are amazing, but I don't particularly want to sit on a plane for four or five hours to see them in the flesh, as it were. Also a friend of mine was chased around the pyramids by a lascivious local and found the whole experience traumatic.

I feel that people get carried away with thinking that being somewhere or doing something will make them happy, and if they can't do it then they are unfulfilled. How do you quantify happiness in the list of different potential scenarios? For me it certainly isn't hanging off the Golden Gate Bridge on a bungee rope, vomiting as I wet myself.

(It's like the long list of unrealistic, unnecessary criteria people put into dating apps: 'I am looking for a beautiful intelligent man with lots of money, three homes, several luxury cars, a sense of humour, a will to succeed and a massive cock.' That's just too much, isn't it? At least have the decency to ask for a small cock.) Throughout our lives, the problem is that we don't get our heads straight and that is what we need to do before saying, 'I must go up the Empire State Building,' or 'I must jump off a massive rock into the sea.' We need to try and facilitate a bit more happiness in our own heads, especially if we are not naturally happy people.

There are various ways to do that.

- Having to be responsible for another person or an animal makes us happy and less selfish.
- Do cognitive behavioural therapy to banish the negative thoughts and replace them with more positive ones.
- Stop reading those crappy books that tell you how to be happy.

- Walk away from people who make you unhappy; it's not that difficult, honestly.
- Be a better friend, listen, support and make your friends laugh more.
- Make an effort, organise days out, charity events and surprise parties and don't expect anything back.

But perhaps one of the main things – taking it right back in a circle – is fulfilling your ambition. If you have not at least tried, you can't have the luxury of moaning about a life unfulfilled.

9

BEING KIND, BEING HELPFUL, BEING GENEROUS . . . ALL THE BLOODY BORING THINGS YOU SHOULD BE DOING

A homeless man came up to me the other day with a beer in his hand. He held out the other hand and in an imploring voice said, '10p, 10p!' So I gave him 10p, took the beer. Bargain.

The results of Stanley Milgram's research conducted in the early sixties shocked the world. In the Harvard psychologist's experiments, ordinary citizens were ordered by lab-coated scientists to administer increasingly powerful electric shocks to other people. These experiments were not intended to demonstrate that humans were fundamentally unkind, rather they were actually set up to see how far people would go in obeying orders. The participants were instructed, looking through a screen at people connected to electrodes, to press buttons that would administer different levels of electric shock if questions were answered wrongly. Most people obeyed the orders to give an electric shock that would easily have been enough to kill without question.

As I said, it was not meant to be a demonstration of how unkind people are, but it is relevant, because if we look at the significant moments in history, during wars, for example – and I know I'm getting a bit serious here – people who behave perfectly normally during peacetime become absolutely out of control and psychopathic. At times of stress, people can often find that their kind nature has deserted them somewhat.

I remember someone I worked with when I was a student, who was quite a senior nurse, saying to me, 'People who treat you like shit, feel that they are shit,' and I think that is important to remember. It doesn't mean that you should initiate an hour of therapy with someone who has just nicked your phone or tried to stab you, but I think it is at the root of it all. People who have suffered the cruelty and unkindness of others normally perpetrate the acts that were perpetrated upon them. This is why kindness is so important.

The job of a social worker arose out of the work of lady almoners – charitable workers attached to hospitals or churches as opposed to lady almonders who picked nuts. The job of social workers eventually became formalised, but to some extent, I think, has retained a slight whiff of a charitable (patronising? moralising?) character, which may contribute to the distaste people seem to have for social workers.

My mum began training as a social worker when I was about ten. She loved her job and initially was based in mental health and then moved on to child protection. I can vaguely remember her going out in the middle of the night to section people and once having to leave a party virtually wearing a ballgown to do the deed. She didn't talk about her job often but when she did, the tales of neglect and cruelty were really appalling and sad and I wondered how she was able to deal with that. Presumably my own move into mental health nursing came in part out of my mum's work but also unconsciously out of some sort of attempt to rectify my dad's poor mental health.

An opportunity presented itself after I was back home having given up the unpopular boyfriend, wanting to go to university but not do a wholly academic course. Brunel seemed the perfect option: a four-year course including nursing training and they didn't care about how shit my A-levels were. I knew I had picked the right course because the vast majority of people training as mental health nurses with me were good, kind but not boring people.

Let's just have a quick look at the reputation of psychiatric nurses. In the past when psychiatric hospitals were closed regimes like villages, it was very easy for an unhealthy ethos to develop and I'm not talking about everyone eating too many chips. Powerful people who had been in the job for many years held sway over the younger ones who were inducted into the regime, which in several places could be cruel and sadistic. (See *One*

Flew Over the Cuckoo's Nest.) Over the years as psychiatric hospitals modernised and let the world in and some people who had lived there for years out, people started to see how institutionalisation had allowed dictatorships to flourish and charities like Mind and Sane began to spring up to protect the rights of those vulnerable people.

I suppose I went into it at a time when the old order was struggling with the new and we had quite a few time-servers who, although not physically cruel on the whole, would tease people and if physical force was required to be used would go in just that little bit too heavily. I believe the more open the institution, the less likely there is to be abuse.

I remember an incident in the Emergency Clinic in which I worked when we were trying to arrange for someone to be admitted under a section. He was a massive guy, tall and very strong, whose worried, scared parents had managed to persuade him to come in. He was what we called, at the time, in the manic stage of bipolar disorder: twitchy, aggressive, thin-skinned, deluded, threatening and hyperactive. The section had been arranged and it was up to me to organise how we would do this. He would not be persuaded to go into a room (two views of this would be that we were secretive and wanted to give him a good kicking OR we preferred to restrain him out of the view of people waiting for appointments in outpatients and it would be less humiliating for him and his family).

Suffice to say the plan went a bit wrong as his strength was superhuman and several of us tussled with him in full view of the waiting throng, including someone from Mind who had come for a meeting and was watching and studiously taking notes (which made me feel guilty even though I wasn't doing anything wrong). Eventually we managed to hold him down on the floor and administer a tranquilliser, trying hard to shield him from embarrassment, and he was taken off to one of the wards. People looked shocked and the Mind person grim-faced.

Then a couple of weeks later the man concerned turned up in our department having been allowed some day release and apologised profusely for his behaviour and everyone gave him a hug. (Those endings don't often get into the frame.)

I think kindness is a difficult thing to teach, even to nurses – like trying to teach someone to be funny. Nurses are supposed to have a 'vocation', a calling to administer love and care to a grateful public, but of course the reality can be very different. All you can do as a senior nurse is keep an eye on everyone's nursing practice and act accordingly.

I mean, how could you sack a nurse for being *unkind*? Impossible, unless they'd slapped someone round the face or hidden their oxygen. Most unkindness comes out of the chronic neglect that happens in nursing and arises from understaffing, exhaustion, management and the fact that the NHS is overseen by bureaucrats and civil servants. It's such a stressful job, though, that you shouldn't do it all your life. After a certain amount of time you can become blunted to people's needs, or cynical, or in some cases rather sadistic. People do snap and they're the ones who make bad psychiatric nurses. You need patience and empathy. Sometimes you only need to give the illusion of control, because if someone is waving a machete, as happened to me once, the worst thing you can do is be a weak heap of begging, because that feeds into the person's feelings of being out of control. They behave worse if they feel they've created chaos. They do all those things that you would quite like to do yourself but you don't because you lose your nerve. They react to every impulse. If they want to throw their house keys off Waterloo Bridge they do it. But however strange their behaviour, a good nurse has to always remember that their patients are still paid-up members of the human race. I'm sorry if I've offended anyone with the word 'patient' – hard habit to get out of. I realise there are better terms these days.

You just have to see through the abuse – and sometimes the smell – and treat them with respect. What matters is not degrees in psychiatry but whether you are a warm human being who wants to help people who are suffering. Many nurses I worked with would give their own money to people who had drawn a blank at the benefits office, bring in clothes from home in case people arrived poorly clothed, or even naked on occasion. The rules were constantly bent or juggled to squeeze out of what was inevitably a mean system the best we could as often as we could.

People always talk about the Good Old Days in a mistily nostalgic way but are things really worse now than they used to be? I think there only seems to be more unkindness around these days because it's so much more visible. I put the blame for that squarely on social media. Who is going to want to upload a little film on to Twitter or MailOnline showing someone giving an old lady a bunch of flowers, when they could show a film of somebody doing something horrible – beating a dog, spitting at someone, or being racist on a train – and get so many more likes? Don't get me started on the hilarity and incongruity of 'likes'! For some reason, we all find anger much more entertaining than kindness. But that doesn't mean we're beyond hope, it just means that we need to work harder at being kind.

The Milgram experiments were inspired by the Nuremberg war trials and the protestations that these people on trial were only obeying orders, simply obeying orders. Then the setting up of the Welfare State was an attempt to try to fuse kindness into the DNA of government.

Governments were urged to take steps to provide citizens with adequate income, adequate health care, adequate education, adequate housing and adequate employment, proposing that 'All people of working age should pay a weekly National Insurance contribution. In return, benefits would be paid to people who were sick, unemployed, retired, or widowed.' The ethos behind this was the stronger helping the weaker. All of our lives have been immeasurably improved by it. And for a long time it worked.

But it's been slowly dismantled here over the last forty years by forces in our society that I would strongly consider to be unkind and, here, I'm not talking about the obvious examples of murderers or criminals. I'm referring to the kind of people who will not give money to beggars, because they assume that actually they've all got massive Georgian houses in Essex that have (of course) been provided for them by the taxpayer. (Why someone with a massive house in Essex would want to come and sit on Waterloo Station in a filthy old blanket and beg every day, I don't know.) But some people use these sorts of stories to justify not having to be kind. These people see the world in a particular way – anyone on benefits is a scrounger and doesn't deserve it; anyone with a disability should not be pandered to; and anyone who is not from a white Aryan race and is resident in this country is some sort of offender – and somehow they seem to be able to excuse this prejudice, for example against immigration, by saying that everyone who wants to live in this country is escaping from a shit nation somewhere else in the world and, basically, their aim is to rob us.

Much of this is based on fear – the sort of fear whipped up to a frenzy by Donald Trump as he takes apart a society blighted by greed and unemployment to replace it with what?

Who knows? Let's come back to it in five years.

All for Charity?

Those who are unkind often defend that unkindness by espousing the argument that there is no such thing as an altruistic act and people who do kind things are only doing them so that they can feel good about themselves. Certainly I'd be lying if I said I didn't get a positive feeling from doing something to help others – but I get a positive feeling from eating a Magnum and from going for a walk. So what? And as for so-called celebrities doing charitable things to advance their careers, who can you think of who was moved up to the next level because they did a benefit or something for Comic Relief? It's *because* they're well known that they're asked to do it FFS.

I started training for the Sport Relief Walk across the top thinner bit of England about a month after my little brother died of stomach cancer. I have no idea where my mind went but it certainly wasn't attached to me for a while. I had always felt like I wanted to take on a big challenge for Sport Relief but as a relentlessly unsporty person with a vague sporting history five hundred years ago at school, I thought that they ought to consider the ranks of the late-middle-aged portly female and include them in challenges. (I had trained many years before for the London Marathon for Comic Relief, although thankfully a virus prevented me doing it, something I was very relieved about as I didn't fancy dropping dead with exhaustion two miles in, dressed as the Isle of Wight.) And although it was announced as my Hell of a Walk I thought if I could do it, it would hopefully raise money while entertaining people watching me struggle frumpily across the English landscape. The fact that the route of the walk was to go from Hull to Liverpool and would go through several places I considered to be forgotten towns also meant a lot to me and I hope something to all the people who came out to greet us, many of whom said nothing like that had ever happened where they lived.

I was trained by the human embodiment of Tigger, an athlete called Greg Whyte. Possessed of boundless energy, the cheeriest demeanour ever encountered in a man and the grumps-expelling talent of a children's nurse, he was the perfect companion in every way. On the entire week-long walk, I think I only got mildly irritated with him once, although when we were training he made me walk up and down Primrose Hill ten times without stopping – a near-death experience in my book. Also as part of the team we had a lovely ex-military geezer called Dot, who used to hit me every night. I believe it's called physio. We also had a doctor called Matt who I had hoped would treat me like Judy Garland: uppers in the morning, downers at night . . . No such luck, it was mainly Paracetamol.

We started the walk on a massive bloody bridge, probably across the Humber, and adrenalin carried me about two miles, I reckon. I don't like heights, so all the way across the bridge I felt slightly panicked and my attempts to smile probably made it look like I'd had a mild stroke.

Each day consisted of pretty much the same routine except the view was different:

5 a.m. Get up and breakfast.
6.30 a.m. Drive to start of day's walk.
6.45 a.m. Start walking.
6.45 a.m.–9 p.m. Walk most of the time interspersed with the odd twenty minutes for food, filming at certain charity projects during the day, getting annoyed with the camera

crew rather unreasonably as for the millionth time the director asked me how I was feeling and made it clear that 'shit' just wasn't good enough.

9 p.m. Get to hotel. Cold bath for ten minutes, physio for half an hour, then hot bath, which I couldn't get out of on the first night owing to being covered in oil. Ended up emptying bath and lining it with towel. More resourceful than I thought.

I realise I was quite bad-tempered but I do think it's fairly reasonable to demonstrate that you have the same moods as other people would have if they were in the same position. There was this teacher who walked along with me at about 6 p.m. and she said, 'Do you mind if I walk with you?' And I said, 'No, I don't mind but I'm in a really bad mood and I might be quite rude to you.' And she said, 'No, that's perfectly all right.' Then she said to me, 'Can I tell my pupils I haven't marked their homework because I'm walking with you?' And when I said, 'Do what you want!' She went, 'How dare you!' and got in a real tizz and walked off. That was the desired result but I thought, Well, I did tell you I was grumpy . . . So I did try to warn people.

Each day a 'celeb' was asked to accompany me and most of them were good mates so that helped: Alan Davies, Bill Bailey, Lee Mack, Gabby Logan, Davina McCall were all roped in and at one stop-off at a primary school I came across Billy Bragg, who sang my favourite song, 'Waiting for the Great Leap Forwards'. If there was ever a moment on telly when I nearly cried (which I steadfastly refuse to do) that was it.

The final day was probably the hardest as we had a very very very long way to go and most of it seemed to be through Liverpool. John Bishop walked the last bit with me and at one point we thought we really weren't going to make it so had to double the pace. Cue second near-stroke.

The festival atmosphere at the finish was pretty overwhelming and it is always at these important moments I find myself dying for a piss and there's nowhere handy to go. I wee-ed in so many fields, forests and bushes on that walk that I feel I watered the whole of the north of England.

On the whole the walk surprised me:

That I finished it.
That I was so grumpy.
That the people on the way were so brilliant.
That we had such a laugh.
That people donated so much money.
That at the end I didn't have ONE SINGLE BLISTER.

Random Acts of Kindness

I do think there is more of a movement to acknowledge kindness these days. I can think of lots of different examples. One of them, of course, is the fashion at the moment for committing 'random acts of kindness', people spending their day trying to do nice things for others. Sometimes it is not very much, maybe only giving someone a bar of chocolate or leaving money to be found somewhere, but personally I think this is a good thing to encourage, especially towards people who are horrible, because that might change their view of the world. I think it's called 'killing them with kindness'. Or perhaps we should just kill them.

Of course random acts of kindness cut out the possibility of being patted on the back. The thinking about doing kind things is that they don't need to be huge grand gestures. Although if you earn a bit you can do a few grand gestures or if you're a squillionaire like Sir Philip Green you can do loads. Still maybe he's saving his pennies to bail the 'hot felon' out of prison. (And if that scenario isn't a glorious indictment of just how risibly shallow our culture is I don't know what is – apart perhaps from Brooklyn Beckham's photography album.)

I would say little acts of kindness are more effective: such as doing a friend's washing-up when they're asleep; making double the amount of dinner and giving half to your neighbour; doing a shift at the food bank. And just being nice to people instead of being grumpy and dismissive; that will obviously involve you being grumpy and dismissive in the first place.

The Importance of Empathy

Empathy is a huge component of being a kind human being because if you can't empathise in some ways you can be a dangerous person because it allows you to treat people cruelly without so much as a thought. Lack of empathy lies along a line beginning with those who just tend to say inappropriate things like 'Sorry to hear you're under the weather,' when you've just had a leg amputated, to those with personality disorders who are very dangerous because of their lack of empathy.

I find some teenage boys have a real lack of empathy and I am presuming it's a huge surge of testosterone, which negates finer feelings in their quest to fight/rob someone/threaten someone – you get the picture. And because all you need is one very dangerous person in one group with the others disguising their misgivings under a veneer of bravado, such gangs can be quite scary. Appealing to a group like that to demonstrate empathy would probably garner some interesting results as you would find many hiding their feelings under a bushel of bravado. Thankfully many teenage boys grow up. The handful that are left who carry on being violent, committing crimes and generally being a great big pain in the arse to society are probably the most damaged by their childhood. Having read the case notes of some very scary people, you will find some absolutely shocking incidents in their childhood and wonder whether they can ever change.

And on that cheery note, complete lack of empathy then ascends up through the floors of humanity passing sadistic teachers, nasty bosses, bullies, neglecters of children and animals until it reaches its optimum level: a sentient human who is able to put himself/herself into the shoes of those who are suffering, which, let's face it, is probably quite a small percentage of society.

The Kindness Police

One of the anomalies in life is that there are certain groups and institutions we expect to be kind, but improved communication has revealed many deep flaws. I think they have lost some of their empathy and listening skills over the years. Let's start with Christians, shall we. The very word implies one is committing acts of such goodness in one's attempts to assist people that fainting from the joy of it all is a possible side effect. Jesus was often caught giving a helping hand to the odd beggar or leper, and, in many ways, he was what we would call a socialist today. Since his followers – quite a few of whom remain to this very day – are supposed to be like him, it is disappointing that so many church-going Christians can be so intolerant. I recall seeing a documentary about people who had given up smoking from the 1930s or 1940s. In it a crowd of people are coming out of church and there is a very sweet little dog standing at the entrance to the church and a guy walks up to this lovely little dog and kicks it up in the air. That's a Christian coming out of church – it's a bit of a give-away, isn't it? (And this of course is without even alluding to the clichéd topic of most of the wars fought through history tending to pit one religion against another.)

We also tend to think of charities as very kind organisations, and it has been revealed recently not always to be the case with many senior members of charity organisations – male members, I might add. I don't need to tell you that joining the Cubs or Scouts and expecting kindness is also not something that kids have always experienced.

We have similarly high expectations of 'carers'. The very name, *carer*, implies that they are looking after someone, doesn't it, but because as a society we seem to have so little respect for carers, and the money is appalling, the job attracts a real array of characters, some of whom, by the law of averages, will abuse their power, particularly if that care home or children's home has developed into an institution in which bullying is an acceptable part of the fabric of the place.

That's not to say that I'm tarring all carers with the same brush. I'm most certainly not. The lengths to which carers will go for a member of their family who has a disability or dementia is really moving. A friend of mine from school became a carer and to hear her talk about it (sometimes she made up to seventeen visits per day) was uplifting. She has now moved back home to look after her own mum and pretty much works all day every day. And this scenario is repeated hundreds of thousands of times throughout the country by an army of people who sacrifice their own ambitions to help others.

The Downsides of Being Lippy

As a feminist and a glass-half-full person, I always expect women to be kinder than men, but obviously that's ridiculous, isn't it? I know a lot of women who are really unkind and a lot of men who are very kind. But I think when women were expected to behave in a certain way, many women put on an act. Now they don't have to do that so much, and they have a little bit more power, we can see new characteristics emerging in women, and being allowed to be expressed, which they certainly weren't some time ago.

For example there are quite a few women in the media who are as hard as fuck and people are terrified of them. I won't say their names just in case I might want to get a teeny bit of work again, but it pains me when we lose another one to the dark side of the moon. I think this all started with Mrs M. Thatcher, who showed you didn't have to be a big softie as a woman and set the wheels in motion for an upward climb in the numbers of 'no-nonsense women', to use a massive euphemism.

I will admit that I have been horrible on occasions, and I have regretted it, but what happens in comedy is that, at times, you get put on the spot to address a heckler, and begin to feel a bit cornered and desperate and something quite unpleasant emerges from your unconscious brain. You think, Oh my God, how on earth did that come out? But it did.

I was hosting *Have I Got News for You* and I told a story when I didn't think the cameras were rolling, about Michael Ball doing a radio show, during which he said, 'We've had a lovely letter from a woman called Helvetica Bond.' Helvetica Bond is in fact a font and he'd made a mistake.

I found this hilarious because it's the sort of thing I would do and have done and repeated the story to the *HIGNFY* audience to entertain them during the break in filming and called Michael Ball 'a knobhead'.

It duly went out on the telly and a few weeks later I was on a show with Michael Ball, whom I have always liked from a distance, and he had seen *HIGNFY* and fixed me with a glare. I felt awful and tried to say I was doing it fondly, which I felt I was at the time. He wasn't having it though. We eventually reached an uneasy truce, but it's a good lesson. You have to stand by what you say and take responsibility for who you have abused, and so it should be.

10

ADVENTURES IN YOUR HEAD

At Swiss finishing school posh girls used to learn deportment by walking round with books on their heads. Feminism might have come a bit quicker if they'd just read them instead.

Interesting, isn't it, that girls completely outperform boys at school and generally do better at most subjects, but as soon as they leave school and head off out into life, that situation seems to reverse and we find ourselves in the land of unequal pay, senior positions in business mainly taken by men, the attitude all over a lot of the media that women are merely decorative and so on, until women are covertly put in their place. (Let's face it, even the supposedly highbrow papers like the *Guardian* and the *Independent*, who should know better, major in front-page pictures of young 'attractive' women compared to older women who have actually achieved something.) In its simplest form this is all about our childbearing facility, which forces us to make choices about the kind of life we want to live, whereas most men feel that family shouldn't impede their striving for the job they want to do and the life they want to lead. Yes, this is a somewhat unfair generalisation and if a backlash was a bull it would be charging towards me now. I'm not going to return to ranty feminism here but I think, generally speaking, some of the problem for women is inside their own heads.

I have repeated the mantra 'Lower Your Expectations' many times, but in the case of women's position in society it should be reversed. I think that many women accept second best in their minds and that dictates where they go with their lives.

So, ironically, women do better at the process of education at school, they are diligent and hard-working, but when converting that into taking the proverbial helm in planning their future they are unable to be as ruthless; they have much less ruth than men do. And women seem to approach the world of work and status in different ways.

Woman Disguised as Man

These women are women who have decided their potential success lies in being more like a man than a man so they appear to have rejected traditional female traits such as co-operation, inclusion and being able to change their mind. Think Margaret Thatcher and 'The lady's not for turning . . .' I still cringe when I think that she probably agreed to say that after a man suggested it.

Woman as Man's Ally

A lot of women come across as very anti other women and constantly express the opinion that modern men are hard done by and disrespected. They often make statements that make them seem harder than men in their attempt to be taken seriously. Think Amanda Platell.

Woman as Siren

Some women use what I think have been traditionally called 'womanly wiles' to operate in our still male-dominated society. So they flirt, flutter and maybe even fuck to make their way in the world. Not giving an example here or I'll get sued, but not me, that's for sure!

Woman as Everyone's Friend

Men will point out that this is an impossible way to operate in any sphere of work if you are a leader. Life, they say, is full of tough choices. But what they don't realise is you don't have to be hard to be human.

Woman as Herself

Eh? I suggest that no one of the female gender ever feels that they can really be themselves and that is our problem. Being a woman and convincing yourself in your own head that you deserve better than you've got, be it an abusive husband or a sadistic boss, is a major challenge. So I'm just going to say what's been important for me.

Books

Reading a book is like retreating into a parallel universe that waits for you whenever you are away from it, and it is so different from films, TV, newspapers, radio, podcasts or any other form of communication. Most people I know who don't read books say that school put them off. The relentless, tedious analysis of character, motive, structure and all the other things that thankfully I've forgotten, which shows how interesting they were. No one is denying that Shakespeare is a fantastic writer, but most kids come out of school basically wanting to shove his winter up his discontent.

If you examine people who are in the media, or have power, or who run huge businesses, you will find that many of them are very well read. But what about Kim Kardashian? I hear you cry. Yes, and I do cry whenever I hear about her. Kim Kardashian is a blip in the business community, as are Katie Price and Posh Spice. But a bloke from a wealthy family, who is privately educated and well read, is not. There are tens of thousands of them, and it is vital that, as much as we all can, we keep up with people like that and we overtake them by fighting them at their own game, and winning.

You can read Shakespeare and comics or you can read *A Brief History of Time* and couple that with Jilly Cooper. You can do whatever you want, but I always try to read widely and use what I read to enlarge my experience of life, of words, of spelling and all those things.

There has been an argument raging recently about whether, if you don't like a book, you should slog on and finish it. Well, in my opinion, limping on to the end of a book about scaffolding may ruin the structure of your brain. Of course, that's not true, but it is important not to waste your time forcing yourself to read something that you don't like, so my advice would be to give up and find something more interesting. When I was at university, I hit my particular wall when I had to read a social theorist called Jacques Derrida. I was cheered to be told by one of my tutors that only a hundred people actually understand his work, because while I was reading it I felt like I was emotionally disturbed. When I looked at the words on the page I couldn't make any sense of them at all. Have a look for yourself, it's good fun, and if you do understand it you are quite worrying, or you're a genius, I'm not sure which. I also like to think it is possible, as so few people understand Mr Derrida, that he might be the one who is emotionally disturbed and in the wrong, not me.

To give you a few statistics about reading: sixteen- to twenty-four-year-olds in this country have lower literacy skills than their equivalents in twenty-one out of twenty-four countries where a survey was done. That means we are lagging behind in many ways as a cultured country. I think a lot of this lack of reading is to do with the way we force schoolchildren to study books that don't have much meaning for them. They probably do have meaning to someone like Michael Gove, who in education terms is two hundred years old, or Jacob Rees-Mogg who is more like a millennium, but if you are going to persuade children to read, you need to find them something they can identify with.

Books offer you whatever you want and I generally have a couple of them on the go at once. I try to have one crappy, easy-to-read novel by my bed, and something a bit more challenging there as well, and I alternate them. So maybe I'll have a Victorian novel or a science book, which makes my brain hurt, next to a fairly standard, gory thriller. A hurty-brain book is a good antidote to all the celebrity magazines like *OK!* and *Heat*, which wash your brain in a sort of fame gunge. (Admittedly I love those too.) Taken together they offer all kinds of ways to look at the world.

My Literary Heroines

My literary heroines tend not to be the traditional ones. I never went for the noble, beautiful, relentlessly marriageable ones whose demure outlook, for me, often washed away their personalities. We are all aware that before a bit of a feminist shake-up, women in novels tended to be decorative future wives, although if they were written by women their characters were slightly more coloured in than the usual park bench with a dress on. For this reason I have eschewed (love that word) the Bennet sisters, Catherine Earnshaw and Becky Sharp.

My top five are:

For grumpiness

Betsey Trotwood in *David Copperfield*
Old, bad-tempered and very kind. I like to think I am all these things except the last one. Outwardly Betsey seems

like a big grump yet her empathy towards David Copperfield outshines the apathy and outright sadism of many other characters in the book. If I'd lived in that era I would have been like her: a resentful, threatening maiden aunt with not a sniff of a wedding in sight.

For cleverness

Jo March in *Little Women*

A seemingly anachronistic heroine, educated, forward-thinking and not obsessed with marriage. '"*Tell another story, Mother, one with a moral to it, like this. I like to think about them afterward, if they are real and not too preachy,*" *said Jo, after a minute's silence.*' My mum named me after this Jo although I hope she wasn't disappointed I never had all my hair cut off to pay for a new fridge.

For taking on unfair systems

Scout in *To Kill a Mockingbird*

Scout was your archetypal tomboy, although it's hard not to see that word fading into the past as the ever more subtle definitions of gender become common parlance. As the only girl in my family, I chose a tomboy's life and fished, climbed trees and didn't wear pink. The fact that Scout didn't really want to be a 'lady' either chimed with me. And then she is at the centre of one of the most powerful books of its era and her reaction and attitude towards the appalling racism prevalent in America at that time for ever seals her into my mind.

For the best arguments

Portia in *The Merchant of Venice*

Of course, the only Shakespeare plays us plebs really know are the ones we did at school. It took me a while to crack on to just how much racism there is in *The Merchant of Venice*, but Portia's magnificent 'quality of mercy' speech shines out of all the darkness, thanks to the brilliant Geraldine James who made me see it in a completely different light in the 1980s. She puts a very persuasive case for choosing mercy over revenge – but unfortunately she's the only woman in the courtroom . . .

For coming back from the brink

Ruth Bryce in *In the Springtime of the Year*

In the Springtime of the Year by Susan Hill is a beautiful book about how we deal with loss. '*They used to say that the birds all stopped singing, for those three hours. That everything went quiet, except for the wind.*' The story of Ruth is eloquent and spare and reads like a long prose poem. This is the most moving evocation of grief (and the dawning of new hope) I have ever read.

Newspapers

We all know that newspaper editors control the opinions printed in their papers.

Paul Dacre of the *Mail* is a good case in point. The *Mail* and what it writes is all about him. He doesn't like fat women who don't look after their appearance (cross against my name), he doesn't like gay people, he doesn't like lefties and I wonder sometimes if he likes anything at all.

Most women read the same paper, if they read one at all, for their whole life because it feeds their views back to them. Get the *Mail*, *Guardian*, *Morning Star* or the *Sun* now and again. See what's happening outside your life.

Politics

I think it's really important as a woman to be interested in politics and to have a clue about what's going on. I still find it hard to believe that lots of people don't recognise pictures of prime ministers. I admire women who start with politics at home, either protesting about work conditions or trying to prevent refuges for victims of domestic violence closing. I have tried over the years to get involved at different levels and it makes you feel like you're doing something, because in a democracy participating means you support it. Who wants to go back to not having the vote?

Use it, for God's sake – you've only got to put a kiss on a bit of paper.

11

FEMINISM: A RE-BRANDING

Apparently MILF means 'Mother I'd Like to Fuck' whereas
MILFO means 'Man I'd Like to Fuck Off'

Growing up as I did in a very small, close-knit community in a village in Kent, I always thought that women and girls were great. Women seemed like a team in our village and I think that's because in those days the tradition of Dad goes to work, Mum stays at home was pretty strong, so you didn't see that many men knocking about during the day. The vast majority of women that I came across were hard-working and humorous whichever background they came from. My mum had very definite ideas about how children should grow up and learn and so TV was limited, reading was encouraged and politeness at all times was drummed into us. My mum decided that when I was a child I should be a child and therefore curtailed anything that beckoned me towards adolescence or would have shaped me into a girly girl. The way this showed itself was by her prohibiting stuff she thought would influence me towards a certain view of the potential life path of women. Looking back at this, it all seems very middle class, doesn't it? Far from it: both my parents came from staunchly working-class backgrounds; both were extremely bright and from youth to their mid-forties metamorphosed from working class to middle class in terms of their outlook, education and earnings.

As a young child I was not allowed to have a Sindy or Barbie doll for the usual reasons: that their ridiculous shape and fantasy long legs said nothing about what women were really like but more what men wanted them to be like. Barbie's unrealistic features include an over-sized head supported by a neck that's twice as long as normal (thus making her 'incapable of lifting her head'), freakishly short arms and a sixteen-inch waist that would only provide for 'half a liver and a few inches of intestine'. Barbie's 3.5-inch wrists would make it extremely difficult for her to lift anything, while her absurdly small feet (the size of an average eight-year-old's) wouldn't be able to support and balance her long frame; she would have to walk on all fours. Let alone her chest–waist ratio, which is physiologically impossible without really extensive plastic surgery and constant dieting. From the very earliest age, girls are given models of female beauty that will always be impossible to achieve.

Oh for God's sake, I can hear some of you think, it's a toy, really, what harm can it do? Maybe the same harm toy guns have had on the psyche of American kids?

I felt hard done by and left out as many of my friends at school cherished their Sindys and Barbies, dressed them up, did their hair and looked as though they felt really sorry for me. I think this was the start of me beginning to feel alienated from the mainstream and growing up to be someone who felt I had different ambitions and a view of the future that was at odds with most of the girls in my class.

The risk you run as a parent if you deny your child the things that most of their peer group play with/read/own is that you do make them feel different and send them off on a different road from that of their fellow travellers.

So I was allowed *Bunty*, a comic for girls that was very old-fashioned and relentlessly uncontroversial and really for girls younger than me, while again my peer group were allowed something I was not: *Jackie*. My mum had a powerful distaste for this magazine, which was all about boys and what girls could do to get boys. So the majority of the features were about make-up, clothes, broken hearts and the like and I was denied a common rite of passage that I have heard many women talk about in later life. I am still not sure whether this was a good thing or a bad thing.

I was the middle child, sandwiched between an older and a younger brother who between them forced me to climb trees and learn how to fight, which it turned out were more useful skills than the traditional feminine ones of needlework or flower-pressing. I was a pretty happy child considering that I was denied stuff that everyone else had but as I blissfully and ignorantly skipped towards adulthood, a massive storm was brewing. Yes, I expect I was a mini-feminist in the making but one who had a long way to go before I clarified in my head exactly what my mother had passed on to me.

I suppose the women I admired when I was younger were also outside the traditional tramlines of society, women who failed to fulfil expectations by settling into the role society felt they should, and I suppose some of those women were women who pushed a feminist agenda. So a woman I admired from a youngish age was Beryl Reid (very funny, independent, seemed not to care what people thought of the roles she took on like *The Killing of Sister George*, which was a pretty scandalous film in its time about the lesbian relationship between two women in the world of television).

Germaine Greer stood out as a difficult woman in a world of mainly co-operative women. Her brand of shocking images and strong ideas shook lots of people up. I guess the realisation of the value of feminism dawned on me when I became aware of the protest at the staging of Miss World in London, hosted by Bob Hope, in 1970 during which a group of feminists threw flour bombs and generally caused mayhem. In those days feminism was called Women's Lib and had the same uneasy relationship with the public that many feminists do. It has gone through many incarnations since. We'll get to those. I think for many women, Germaine Greer and this protest at the time was a bridge too far. Most women I imagine didn't feel ready for something quite as radical as Women's Lib and although I suspect many of them were uneasy about the situation of women, throwing flour and what with

Germaine Greer talking about cocks ... It was all a bit too controversial for most.

Many women feel similarly today about feminism because the effective PR campaign waged against it over the years has made them feel that women who support a feminist agenda are aliens who are intellectual and middle class and nothing to do with them. That has changed to some extent with Girl Power – a sort of feminism – and the work of women like Caitlin Moran who have tried to be inclusive rather than separatist.

One thing that does drive me mad is when women are called 'ladies'. It implies a feminine subservience, an obsession with appearance, a waiting to be manoeuvred, a weakness, a quietness. I've had to stop myself from shouting, 'It's WOMEN!' many times. It matters to me!

The Rights of Women

I don't feel I have ever had to really speak to my daughters about feminism formally, as they have kind of imbibed it without me having to sit them down in front of a visual aid and tell them the whole story with a big pointy phallic symbol. Young women these days seem to espouse the kind of feminism that is summed up by 'I don't take any bullshit,' but many of them continue to, if individual stories are anything to go by. Add in the mix of cultures in big cities and the differing degrees of freedom accorded, and there is a huge variation in the opportunities afforded young women. And we haven't even touched on class and education.

One area that does worry me is the student lifestyle where parties and freshers' weeks seem beset with Neanderthal male students joining shag-a-fresher shenanigans or publicly treating women like lesser beings and student unions seem a bit slow to condemn it. Occasionally, it's easy to see the gains that have been made by the women's movement converted back into losses. Let's just remind ourselves:

Married women once were men's property and so was their property.
Women couldn't go to university.
Women couldn't vote.
Women had no opportunities to use contraception.
Women earned (and still do) substantially less than men in certain areas.

But also that women's silence about and co-operation with differing levels of sexual harassment and assault in a wide variety of institutions from charities to the BBC have allowed many men over the years to get away with criminal acts.

Feminists are often accused of being humourless and anyone who's just read the last page will probably find themselves agreeing with that.

Plus, the language of feminism has always put people off, because it is necessarily left-wing and intellectual, and because the sort of people who write about feminism are academics, which I believe makes the vast majority of the female population feel alienated from it. We all know what we think is acceptable, but it depends on what sort of language we want to be applied to feminism. Feminism should be discussed in the language of the people not the language of a professor of sociology. I think that Girl Power was an attempt to do this but it kind of fizzled out and wasn't sustainable in the long run because it was a bit gimmicky and seemed to be more about the Spice Girls selling records rather than a real sense of addressing normal women who were struggling.

Also, in order to straddle the different generations I think it's important to have a nuanced sort of feminism that doesn't feel like it only applies to a certain age group. Is the F word a busted flush? I can't help feeling that in some ways it is. The press have waged such a war against feminism for so long that the images they have created have settled in people's heads.

My view about feminism is that it should be a broad church that includes everyone who thinks women have got a raw deal, and that stretches from your lap dancers all the way through to your university professors. The problem I always had was that I looked like a radical feminist, but in reality I was a slightly lipstick feminist in many ways. If you don't know what a lipstick feminist is, it's someone who broadly believes in feminist principles, but wants to wear alluring clothes and make-up rather than look like one of Chairman Mao's workers. To me it means not being berated for, on occasion, compromising a bit rather than Punish! Exclude! Separate! (Sounds like a particularly harsh sports bra.) There are lots of men I like and some of them are even a bit sexist. Rome wasn't built in a day. Chill. And while we're on the subject I hate the word 'empower'. I can't help it, it just sounds like it was invented by a wanker for wankers and has become attached exclusively to the women's movement. If we shared it around a bit with people on zero-hours contracts or modern-day slaves it might lose some of its wanky-ness.

And while we're on the subject, 'Lean In' drives me nuts as well, because I think again that was invented by a very senior business person who doesn't know what it means to live a normal life. To me buzzwords or phrases just pointlessly skim the surface of meaning and don't really help but just paper over the cracks.

Types of Feminists

- Suffragettes: Emmeline Pankhurst types (more middle class/better hats); Sylvia Pankhurst types (more left-wing/lived in East End).
- Separatist feminist man-haters (a massive cliché and suspect there are only about three in the country).
- Academics (have sort of lost the connection with real people).
- Politically active feminists (women who have time to do it, i.e. not any kids under the age of twelve).
- Seventies bra burners (only women with small bosoms).
- Girl Power devotees (no comment).
- Armchair feminists (my favourite).
- Part-time feminists (when it suits).

- Lipstick feminists (want their cake and eat it; well, what's wrong with that?).

Everyone else who thinks women should be equal (the rest, many women who haven't even thought about it that much).

Time's Up and Me Too. People moan that all these smug actresses didn't have to do much to support these movements. But it's a fuck of a lot more than any group of men in Hollywood have ever managed.

Everyday Sexism 101

Everyday sexism is a term coined by Laura Bates to identify those fleeting acts (up to massive, breathtaking acts) of sexism that you hardly notice but that can be identified as differentiating between men and women and subtly disempowering (weird – I don't mind it with a 'dis' on the front) women in relation to men.

Have a look on their website, it's fascinating.

Top Five Sexist Lines and How to Counteract Them

Show us your tits; maybe a variation inviting you to do it 'for the lads'.
Where's your girlfriend then? In a field grazing?

Cheer up, love, it may never happen.
Keep talking and it will.

Women are crap at parking.
That's because men have small knobs (a play on the well-known joke: that's because for years men have been saying 'that's ten inches').

You obviously hate men.
No I don't, it's just you.

You need a good shag.
I'll look elsewhere then.

What's Not Working and How Can We Fix It?

So if feminism is such a great idea, why is there so much disagreement about what to do? The problem with so many different branches of feminism is like that of political parties that are split in several ways: no one ever gets anything bloody well done, because they are always arguing with each other. This is evident in the way that different groups of women feel that they have been excluded from the feminist movement, and rightly so in some cases – black women, for instance, or women with a disability. If there was a room big enough to put them all in, they could talk it out until they came to some sort of compromise. For compromise is what is sadly lacking in this day and age between every political group, and rather than attacking each other over their differences, they should talk about them.

This is also a way to settle the ongoing row between feminists and trans women, because there is a lot of disquiet over the new rules about trans women. These rules are concerned with self-identification as one or other gender, and in certain arenas it is considered adequate to self-identify and be permitted access to areas that have been traditionally exclusively male or female. The trouble is that as soon as a feminist stands up and says that they feel uneasy about it, trans activists go on the attack. Nothing gets agreed upon and feminists are either shut down or excluded from speaking – no-platformed, I believe it's called – and that isn't getting us anywhere whatsoever. There's even been a term coined for extreme feminists who are challenging the rules about trans people: they are called Terfs, trans exclusionary radical feminists, whereas I like to think of myself more as a surly mother understudying radical feminists – or a Smurf. Can we relax, stop being aggressive, employ some humour and humility and stop jumping down each other's throats? The argument always seems to go from 0 to 60 in 2 seconds.

Added to which, not all women like the idea of feminism. I met very few girls or women who were horrible when I was young, and I assumed that women were naturally supportive of each other. Of course, as life marches on and I get older, I realise it is not quite that simple and I have come to understand that the sisterhood doesn't include quite as large a percentage of the female popula-tion as I had believed.

I went to three different schools when I was a kid – a primary school, then two secondary schools – and at none of these schools was bullying by girls evident. It may well have been going on and I was oblivious to it, but now my eyes are opened a little more and I have come to the conclusion that many women don't like other women; I wouldn't want to put a percentage on it, but hey, let's live dangerously – 20 per cent?

Quite a number of women are also bullies – again shall we risk a percentage, say 5 or 10 per cent – and many of these women consciously support men whose behaviour is unacceptable, if not downright perverted. How else do you explain the millions of women in America who chose not to see what was going on in front of their eyes with Donald Trump, and even though he made such bald statements as saying he grabs women by the pussy, they still thought he was okay in a kind of 'huh! – men will be men' kind of way? And the country's attitude towards Hillary Clinton and her earnest hard-working preachiness made things worse. One of the saddest things about the election results was seeing the lengths that Hillary's team had gone to to find a venue with a glass roof for their victory party so that she could make a killer gag about smashing the glass ceiling in her victor's speech. Ah, the dangers of a long build-up to a punchline.

If you listen to women who were employed in big institutions where misogyny, sexism and abuse were rife in the seventies – and let's take the BBC as our example, because there was a lot of it going on there, with the likes of Mr Savile and various others – many of them look down on younger women today as wimps, who should just put up with being groped and propositioned, or having their chests tweaked in a *Carry On* kind of way.

It saddens me that they are not pleased that younger women are managing to claw back some more power and control. But I do understand where their anger is coming from. Many older women are really grumpy because, looking back, they realise they have lived a life that has not fully satisfied them. They are envious of the opportunities and potential younger women have today. But then my mother's generation were envious of us in turn. It's called progress – and we need to suck it up.

Feminism at Work

Feminism can flourish or die in the workplace depending on what your work is and what your boss's attitude is. Some City-type places make ridiculous demands on women at work like they have to wear heels and are only permitted to wear the colours of lipstick that are displayed on a card.

Men feel threatened by women invading male-dominated space and quite a lot of men are stoopid enough to go on about it in emails and that's how we find out. How could you not be a feminist when you read about the sorts of things trolls say to women in the public eye? And you've probably seen the pictures of the woman at work who was taped into a chair by male colleagues for something pretty innocuous. There's clearly still a lot of progress to be made.

In comedy, I certainly experienced no overt misogyny

from other acts although audiences made up for that in spades. I was once doing a pretty rowdy gig and a man down at the front got on the table, flopped out his flaccid penis and shouted, 'Suck my dick, you fucking bitch,' at me. Despite the fact I could have tried variations on the electron microscope put-down I didn't see why I had to put up with this, so I walked off – and I got reprimanded for coming off stage two minutes early!

Luckily for me I had had many difficult experiences as a mental health nurse, the difference being that in comedy you're allowed to answer back and I relished the challenge most times. Obviously I've had far worse things said to me at work than most people, like, 'I want to ram a table leg up your cunt.' I'm always disappointed I can't find that charming sentiment on something in a card shop.

The sort of abuse women get demonstrates how much of an underground misogyny movement of real hatred there is, not to mention the surface examples from Trump to football managers, and this is what women are up against. I'm hoping this historical hatred of women will die out as I genuinely believe a lot of young men these days are a huge improvement on the gobby walking sacs of testosterone around in my day. I'd like to see a few more men supporting the women's movement rather than all the ones who have said Harvey Weinstein's not such a bad geezer after all. Perhaps feminism does need rebranding and along with the current hoo-hah about pay and sexist abuse things are moving in the right direction.

We've got to stop being so British about pay and men have got to start being more supportive of women without thinking they've been de-testicled. A lot of men live this double life of paying lip service to feminism publicly then getting stuck into a nice touch of violent hardcore porn when the lads come round.

Feminism at Home

In a nutshell, is it a move forward to go from women doing 80 per cent of the housework to men and women both doing 20 per cent and thereby leaving 60 per cent of the housework not completed? I think so. Let's all live in a dump and be equal. The lack of parity in most homes is because women carry the 'emotional load' for running the house, an idea that started in France. This describes the intimate links in the chain of how to run a household which include such diverse issues as dog needing worming, where to go on holiday, school clothes needing replacing, washing required for the next day, batteries being replaced in smoke alarm – things most men are not aware of and women end up taking on. Suggestions on a postcard please!

How Many Feminists Does It Take to Change a Lightbulb?

Do it yourself, you lazy bastard.
Or
Just the one but she's fucking fuming.

Or

Let's not bother, seeing as you're still living in the Dark Ages.

Or

Yes, of course I know how to change a fucking lightbulb.

And so on . . . to infinity and beyond – well, let's hope not.

Heckle Put-Downs for Power

The Nottingham police record misogyny as hate crime and are stunned by the prevalence of criminal acts towards women, while at universities there has been a rise in really nasty attitudes towards women expressed in events like rag week; and anyone just needs to look online to see how women are targeted by Neanderthal tossers hiding behind anonymity.

One response that works very well is if you just say, 'Could you repeat that, please?' Normally only one idiot in five is prepared to reiterate whatever childish remark they have made.

A handy list of retorts for all occasions:

Oh, I'm sorry, I mistook you for a human being.

I think you'll find most males stopped making remarks about women's chests/bums when they were ten years old.

Did you mean to make such an offensive and infantile remark?

All these things bear practice before you need to use them so they come out confident, controlled and unfazed.

And that's what we're aiming for.

Staying a Feminist

Lots of people as they age change political allegiance from left to right.

Is this similar for feminists? How many of them end up in the WI tutting at Tony Blair and eating handfuls of jam straight from the jar?

It's important to keep the enthusiasm going; although once a feminist, always a feminist, you are unlikely to take a career break from feminism and devote your time to the care and nurturing of a Tory MP. (This won't go down well at Cheltenham.)

There are still quite a few myths about feminism. 'You don't get any pretty feminists,' is one of them. Well, obviously I am a living proof that is not the truth. Another is that feminists aren't funny, but there are hundreds of women comics out there who are feminists and are funny, so thbbpthbpt!* to that.

Madeleine Albright, the American politician, once said there is a special place reserved in hell for women who don't support other women, and I support her in making

---

* My evocation of a raspberry.

that statement, because I think we need to get more women and men on board the Good Ship Feminism, rebranded or not, and move her off the sandbank into waters new.

(And don't get me started on ships being named after women.)

12

MODERN MANNERS

Do you find that when you're in a restaurant and your partner's meal arrives you want that? Not instead, as well.

I may have done the voiceover for a series called *Ladette to Lady*, but that's where it stopped. I am not going to be talking about balancing books on your head or which fork to use, because that outdated concept of etiquette is long gone, apart from in about three Georgian mansions in Mayfair, I would imagine. I want to talk about good manners, and rather than trawling my way through every aspect of social interaction, I have picked the areas of life in which I think people could do with much better behaviour.

Home Etiquette

Okay, let's start with being at home. When I was growing up certain behaviour was expected of us at certain times of the day and I suppose there were vague echoes of a

Swiss finishing school in the 1930s, but pared down to the practicalities, so we didn't have our knives, forks and spoons lined up in a particular way or arrange the staff in order of height and weight.

At mealtimes, it was expected everyone would sit at the table for most meals. (When my mum went out to work this relaxed a bit because I was responsible for producing something resembling a meal. I achieved this by not actually cooking anything but assembling a wonky ploughman's on a big plate that we then ate while watching telly. Sacrilege. This became known as 'tea on a plate' and barely changed its contents for years.)

However, when we all ate together these were the rules:

1. No chewing with your mouth open.
2. No reading at the table.
3. No food allowed to be left on plate. I was once coerced into eating a gooseberry pie my mother had made when I was about six years old. (I abhorred gooseberries and think it stemmed from that joke, 'What's green and hairy and goes up and down?' 'A gooseberry in a lift.' Just couldn't get that 'hairy' thing out of my head.) Anyway, the gooseberry pie reappeared fairly soon after when I vomited it all over the stairs. (Strangely enough that was the last time gooseberry was on the menu.)
4. No one allowed to eat after my mum had finished her meal. (I'm joking but I believe this is what happens with the Queen.)
5. Children have to ask to leave the table by saying, 'Please can I get down?'

6. No elbows on the table – though we were not the sort of family that had serviettes on the table in a three-sided container (I've seen silver ones) or a spoon *and* fork for pudding, which we did not call 'sweet'.
7. No second helpings before guests.
8. If you're at someone else's house, don't make a face if you don't like the food – and eat it all up. That final word 'up' always has to be used when you're talking to children.

When I was under the age of five, I was invited in to the next-door neighbour's. She was very elderly – let's say she'd given up housework quite a long time before, it was very hot, her kitchen was smelly and the general food hygiene was not good. To my horror she offered me a drink from a bottle of warm long-life milk, which was standing on the table and had several flies on it and round it. She poured the milk into a dirty cracked cup. My stomach heaved and everything in me told me not to touch it, but an image of my angry mum bounced up and down in my head. I took one sip, said I was late for tea and ran all the way home projectile-vomiting as I went.

Other Rules

1. Always say 'please' and 'thank you'.
2. Write thank you letters after birthdays and Christmas – and not just the sort of cursory message that says, 'Thanks for the "thing", love Jo'.
3. Give up your seat for an older family member.
4. Don't eat all the nice biscuits when people are round for tea.
5. Send postcards.

Breaches of family etiquette were swiftly and forcefully pointed out with no nod to the potential this had for the embarrassment of the offender, which I suppose made reoffending unlikely.

I think that for many families this century, the rules have been relaxed enormously. Compared to the above list that controlled my childhood home I have rather fewer rules, although there is a minimum standard in our house.

- No putting your feet up on the cats.
- Don't eat with your bowels open.

Sorry, I'll stop this right now. Suffice to say – decent behaviour at the table. No phones unless I'm using mine . . .

I couldn't care less which body parts they put on the table unless it's . . . no, I mustn't go there. But they don't have to ask to leave the table or clear their plates of food. I normally do that. With my mouth.

To be honest, I couldn't care less if table manners are not perfect as long as my family members treat each other with respect. So, any food throwing has to be cleared up by the culprits themselves.

The following are what I consider to be bad manners:

1. Children who say, 'Eugh, I don't like that.' They can bugger off home. That doesn't work with my own kids unfortunately.
2. Children who don't say please and thank you.
3. Children who don't send a thank you note when I have said hello to them in the street.

While we're on 'please and thank you', I have spoken to a lot of people who feel the same as me, which is that if you stop to let someone pass, either driving or walking – is it a middle-class thing to do? I don't know – I like it if people say thank you. This is why women are nicer than men, because a straw poll that I have taken myself over the years indicates that men say thank you about one in ten times and women do so about six out of ten, which leads me to think that women are the politer of the species. Women are just more helpful and maybe that's a manners thing and the fact they don't have to feel they need to keep up some sort of bulletproof front to demonstrate they're hard as fuck. This front in many men is watered and maintained by testosterone and allows them never to be seen to be weak. Let's just dispense with some other bad manners.

Selfishness

There are many selfish people who are never challenged about their drive to ensure their entire life is arranged for their own benefit. I am presuming this started in their families, but now they are adults they need to be challenged – to a fight if possible. I have some friends who come round and talk about themselves for hours on end and more recently I've found myself out a lot of the time when they've threatened to drop by. One question *not about* themselves every seven minutes would bring me back home.

Helping and Sharing

People who don't help out and/or share should be executed.

White Lies

Fine by me if they save someone's feelings.

Guest Behaviour

Due to post-menopausal grumpiness, I prefer it if guests don't come in the first place.

If they do, can they not sit there like a huge mouth on the settee expecting something to be shovelled in every two hours.

Mobile Phone Etiquette

Not in the cinema, theatre, in a shop especially while paying for goods, in a train carriage at twenty decibels, not in church, not in a comedy club, during an exam, while visiting a relative in hospital, while having sex, during a gynae exam, a child's school play, on take-off, on landing. In fact just in your own in a lead-lined box.

The same goes for the playing of video games apart from perhaps in church if the sermon is boring (and I don't even go to church).

ROAD RAGE (mostly mine)

Driving is interesting: it takes all this etiquette obsession into a much smaller space and amplifies its effects – hence road rage. We've all been in a car when the driver's head explodes at a minor infringement taking place on the road in front of them. Often it is an extremely petty thing, but people can go from o to 60 in no time at all. (I'm afraid I am one of them.) It is terrible to admit, but driving these days feels increasingly like a video game. Sometimes I wish I really was in a game, and could blow up the car in front of me when it is driving me nuts.

People are generally less polite behind the wheel of a car. Take when there is a queue of traffic and you let people into it. You get your arsey kind of lad in a powerful car, who will just move into that space and every fibre of his being screams 'fuck you'. On a number of occasions I have fantasised about getting out of my car and giving them a good old-lady ticking-off. Yes, I know I would probably get punched into a hedge, but I would still love to do it.

Likewise when you see police-car lights or an ambulance in your rear-view mirror, and virtually everyone pulls into the side of the road to let them pass, and then – this has happened to me many times – some twat in a massive 4x4 is behind you, aware that you have pulled over as well, then overtakes you and zooms off in front of you. Again, I have fantasised about catching them up and scraping my key down their paintwork at the next traffic lights. I have so very many exotic fantasies when I am driving.

I do not like tailgating on the motorway. I also don't like being flashed when I am not going fast enough. (Headlights not penises.) If I've got room to pull in and someone is coming up behind me at 200 miles an hour, I will pull over, and most people will. I also can't stand people who hog the middle lane and I always feel guilty when I go past them with evil thoughts in my head, because normally it turns out to be a sweet old lady, or a family who look like they don't have a clue where they are going, and my crossness melts away.

I do a lot of motorway driving on tour. I always drive myself because I prefer it, but once I was trying to get into Watford Gap services, desperate for a wee, and I pulled into the middle lane from the fast lane and there were three lorries travelling together in the slow lane in a little group, and they conspired not to let me in to Watford Gap. I have no idea why they did this, and I had moved ahead of them by that time, so I couldn't be bothered to slow down and shake my fist at them, which is my preferred method of protest, because it makes other people in the car laugh as well.

I have been the victim of road rage on one or two occasions and I have to admit it was probably my fault. One time, looking for somewhere to park, I was driving quite slowly. I could see the woman behind me getting increasingly frustrated. When I did manage to pull in somewhere, she pulled up next to me, winding down her passenger window, and giving me a right earful. I couldn't help myself. I upped the ante and gave her worse abuse back and then I took off.

She chased me for about half an hour and it got quite scary. I was hoping we weren't going to get to that point where we got out of our cars and had to have a fight, because she did look much tougher than me. But luckily for me, she hadn't done rally driving and I had. I did that thing of slowing down at the traffic lights and then, as they turned red, shooting through them and leaving her behind. It was like something out of a film (*Chariots of Fire*) and incredibly satisfying. I know, that's awful, isn't it – not least in a chapter where I am trying to encourage you to be nicer to each other – but I'm the first to admit that behaving well doesn't always come easily. I am not proud of being an aggressive driver, and normally I am not, if people drive properly, but it brings out the homicidal headmistress in me. I think, How are people going to learn, unless we tell them off all the time? So I see that as my job, which I know is ridiculous.

Tipping

What sort of people do we tip? What do they all have in common?

That's right, people who offer us a service and people who earn shit wages.

Why would you not tip? Use the principle of the widow's mite in the Bible (search engine ahoy). What you can afford to tip is perfectly all right and just as valuable as some rich tosser giving someone a huge amount. If you are on the telly, don't ever tell a journalist what a huge amount you tipped someone once. It makes you look like a knob.

Fly Tipping

Leaving big piles of flies at the side of the road along with furniture, old prams and the inevitable wrecked shopping trolley is totally unacceptable. Punishment for someone should be seventy Rottweilers shitting in their garden for a year.

Queue-bargers

Moving on to queuing, I don't like people pushing into queues, and I don't like it when people are queuing and then fifteen of their friends turn up and they say, 'Oh, I've saved a place for you.' Also, we've all done it. When you get stuck behind the person in a post office who has twelve parcels, you might think, 'Fair enough, it is all right to do that'. But what I don't like is when they have done their twelve parcels after ten minutes and you think, 'Thank God, they've finished', and then they make an enquiry about something else that takes another ten minutes. By which time the rest of us are all banging our heads on the wall.

Parties

Secretly no one likes parties that much:

- Don't take the most expensive bottle of wine from the table, leave your crappy bottle of Sainsbury's finest and go home.
- Don't put your fag out on the carpet.
- Don't have sex in the bedroom (unless you're under sixteen in which case you can't do it because it's against the law).

Small talk at parties can be excruciating so try a few more exciting openers:

- What's the most violent incident you've ever witnessed?
- Do you know anyone at this party who's had sex with my husband?
- I've been in prison, have you?
- Which member of the Conservative Party would you most like to shoot?
- What's the worst lie you've ever told?

Cyclists, Dog-Owners and Pram-Pushers

There are unspoken laws of the pavement that cyclists and people who are concentrating on looking after something else, pushing a baby along in an enormous space-age pram or walking a dog, feel at liberty to ignore. I can understand a mother with three kids under the age of ten cycling on the pavement, but if they are going to do that, they need to realise they are in the wrong place and give way to the people who are going along using their feet. So if you must, cycle on the pavement, but don't try and take control of it, because we are the pedestrians and that is our territory. The same goes for dawdling pairs of middle-class mothers blocking up pavements with their enormous space-age prams, as they gaze enraptured at their phones rather than their children. I have often seen them, deliberately ignoring the little old ladies trying to get past them.

But worst of all are the dog-owners who don't give a shit (or rather those who leave the shit on the pavement for all of us to walk through). Dog poo is revolting and quite dangerous, and it is just horrible. I live in an area where the vast majority of people do pick it up, because of the accusatory glances of the locals, and there is an equation. The scarier and bigger the dog, the less likely its poo is to be retrieved by the owner and there are no accusatory glances at these sorts of people owing to the locals not wanting to die. I think that is simply the way it is. Good manners are great but discretion is most definitely the better part of valour.

Rubbish

Big or small littering is another thing I abhor. There are lots of things I don't abhor, like in the Christmas carol 'Oh come all Ye Faithful' I do not abhor the virgin's womb either. Recycling is a brilliant idea. But it really pains me to go and recycle stuff, only to find that a local builder has just poured two tons of rubble next to the plastic recycling. What the fuck have they done that for? I also hate people who drop litter and that is an issue, isn't it, because do you or do you not challenge someone who looks like they have just done a twelve-stretch when they drop some paper on the pavement?

The sensible answer is no, you don't, in case they don't like it and they wrap you round a lamppost.

The Art of Travel

Any kind of travelling involves frustrated, angry people, and therefore normal etiquette is not observed, but I would say on a plane it is not very polite to be pissed out of your head for the entire flight. That is something that people could improve on. It is also not very polite to put your seat back as far as it will go and give the woman behind you a hysterectomy, so that is another thing. I don't like people who put their feet on the seats on trains, but unfortunately by the law of averages people who do that are not going to say, 'Oh certainly, I had no idea I was offending you,' when you ask them to put their feet down. They are more likely to do something alarming, so that is another minor crime that goes unpunished.

By the way, I am well aware that I sound like the Tory candidate for Weston-super-Mare and I feel bad about it, because while politically I am still left-wing, manners-wise I have swung over to the far right. I regret it in some ways, I enjoy it in others.

Good manners are important and it is a pity they are called good manners because the ears of the vaguely fascistic immediately prick up as they contemplate how much the country has gone downhill since immigrants arrived.

Good manners, to give them a more contemporary spin, are just about us respecting each other and giving people space to be individuals, while not running riot and encroaching on all our personal zones.

So think about treating people as you would like to be treated, apart from the roads where all bets are off.

Only kidding.

13

KEEPING SAFE

I got a text from my writing partner once that said, 'I'm sending the rapist round in a cab.' What???? When the cab arrived it turned out to be a script. Bloody predictive texting.

It seems as if almost every month we are served up a new horror, whether it is an increase in knife crime or teenage boys on scooters snatching mobile phones; stalking appears to have sky-rocketed numbers-wise; and a recent addition to criminal behaviour is a huge increase in acid attacks. In fact the dangers are far less than they were in the past, when women were considered to be even more disposable. Back in those days, villages, towns and cities were not lit at all, and criminals and rapists could go about their business without too much trouble. The world is slowly improving and becoming safer for women but it's not there yet. I have done a lot of risky things in my time and having two daughters has made me look back on my life very differently. I actively do not want any other women to get into similar situations and luckily there are some practical solutions (interspersed with some stories of my near misses) that I hope will inspire you to be more sensible than I was.

Prepare for the Worst, Hope for the Best

In an ideal world, all women would be able to afford a cab if they were coming home late at night on their own. Obviously, there is a big difference safety-wise between towns and rural areas. It is pretty risky as a woman on your own to walk home along a dark country road at night.

When I was much younger, determined to go out but with little or no money to get back home at the end of a night, I sometimes hitch-hiked although my mother had always pleaded with me not to. You've heard one hitch-hiking horror story already but this was the near miss that made me change my tactics. I was given a lift by a squaddie, whose mental health turned out to be not that great. He drove me down a dark lane in the middle of nowhere in an area I didn't know at all, and then stopped the car and turned to me. My blood really did literally seem to run cold, my hands were freezing. I decided I had nothing to lose and I screamed at him as loudly as I could, 'What the fuck are you going to do now?' Much to my relief, he burst into tears, and told me how bad things were for him, and then he drove me back to where I was staying. But that could have gone down a terribly different route and he could have got away with it. (As recently as 1983 a male judge simply fined a male taxi driver who had pleaded guilty to the rape of a seventeen-year-old hitch-hiker £2,000 because 'she was guilty of a great deal of contributory negligence',* i.e. in non-legal language she was asking for it, which is such rubbish that even Margaret Thatcher tried to get the judgment overturned.) I then decided that if I was left with only the choice of going home very late on my own, I would stay at someone's house.

Even if extra safety measures are a hassle and irritating, they are better taken than ignored. There are a few sensible things you can do.

Always be aware of your level of consciousness when you're on a night out. Opportunists are looking for women who are off their face on one thing or another, because they tend to make poor judgements about how to handle themselves. All we have to do is look at the career of John Worboys. He was a black cab driver. Black cabs are always touted as being safe places for single women, but Worboys would offer women drugged champagne, and then attack them at will, because their level of consciousness was not enough for them to fight back.

- Never be afraid to speak up or say no.
- Never accept a drink from any man you don't know, and especially not in a pub if you have not watched that drink actually being poured from a bottle or a pump.

---

* Another high court judge, Sir Melford Stevenson, strongly agreed: 'It is the height of impudence for any girl to hitch-hike at night . . . She is, in the true sense of the word, asking for it.' Arrgh!

- Never leave your drink unattended.
- If you are drinking out of a bottle, cork it, so that no one gets a chance to slip anything into it.

Please be vigilant. What young women have to do is to assume the worst. I know that is a terrible indictment of society, but it means you will be a lot safer.

Don't Freeze, Look For Help

One thing that has always held women back from responding to any unwanted advances is the paralysis that happens when you are very fearful. I was once on a Tube coming in to London, when I was a student, and a guy sat down opposite me. It was fairly late at night and the Tube was almost empty. He had a book on his lap and slowly I realised without looking directly at him that he was masturbating.

I didn't have the confidence to say, 'Can you put that away,' or make some sarcastic comment about what he was doing. In the end, I got up and walked down to the end of the carriage to where there was a couple sitting together. I explained what was going on, and asked for their help, but they looked at me as if I was completely mad and ignored me. So that resulted in me getting off at the next stop and waiting until another train came along with a slightly more crowded carriage.

It is obviously disappointing when 'members of the public' don't help you, but you have got to expect this, because people are often quite unpredictable. They don't want to get involved, in case they might be in some danger. So, if you think you're not going to be helped, move on and try to find help elsewhere.

As nurses, in dealing with the threat of violence, we were taught that if at all possible, leg it. Also, if you are going to scream, call out something neutral like 'Fire!'. It's sad but true that people are far more likely to respond to this.

There's Safety in Numbers

There is undoubtedly safety in numbers, so groups of friends need to talk to each other about this when they go out. They need to be absolutely sure that at the end of the evening they don't let one of their crew stagger off into the darkness, leaving themselves extremely vulnerable, *whatever* they say to you. That is really important. If you are in a situation in which someone is being harassed or appears to be in a dangerous situation, obviously it's scary but just acknowledging it will sometimes put people off what they are doing.

My mum did this once on a Tube when she noticed three young guys harassing and touching a young woman while everyone else studiously looked the other way. Bloody humans – don't they realise if they all ganged up they could stop it? My mum just said, 'Are you okay?' and the girl replied, 'No, not at all,' so my mum told the boys to leave her alone, got a mouthful of really appalling abuse, but they did leave the girl alone.

I once saw a man and woman arguing furiously in Camden and thought he was going to hit her, so walked up and said, 'What the fuck are you doing?' He was so astonished, he turned to look at me and while he was doing this, the woman hit him on the head with her umbrella.

Alternatively you could make a call to the police and at least you will be seen to be doing something.

Be Prepared

If anything is going on and you are boxed into a corner by someone, you need to have the confidence to make a fuss about it. I have always found that one way of doing this is to rehearse scenarios in your head. It is not very pleasant, I understand that, but it stands you in good stead. Ask yourself, what if . . . and put yourself in that position. Think what you would do, so that if it ever happens to you, it is not completely unexpected and you can probably react more quickly than you would do otherwise.

Another thing I have always done, if I am walking home on my own and I am a little bit nervous, is to wrap my fingers around the sharpest key in my bunch, so that should I have to, I can give them a good poke in the eye with it. Again, I'm sorry, I know none of us want to be doing a key-enabled dissection of the eyeball late at night, but these situations require some fairly drastic action, unless you are someone who has done judo and you are particularly flexible at kicking someone in the bollocks.

You need to have other options, such as a rape alarm – they are brilliant, they make a very loud noise – or it might be a faceful of your favourite perfume. That sort of thing does work, and it gives you a chance to leg it. Predators are looking for things in your situation to take advantage of; look for the things that could help you escape. Be prepared.

As a stand-up I always found verbal put-downs useful; just to have a few up your sleeve for flashers, wankers and general perversion-mongers.

Flashers

No thanks, I don't smoke.

That looks like a penis only smaller.

Can't quite see what that is. I should have gone to Specsavers.

Animal, mineral or vegetable? I like that game.

Maybe try Tinder first?

Hmm, don't get many of those to the milligram.

Masturbators

Wanker alert, everyone!

Can you stop doing that, I'm trying to concentrate on my book.

Can you put that away, it might shrivel up in the cold – oh, it already has.

Bloody hell, that's *tiny*!

Or just try screaming; it's always effective and gives them a shock.

Trust Your Instincts
(Unless, of Course, You Are Very Drunk)

If something feels wrong, it is wrong. I think women are bad at doing this but it's got me out of trouble more than once. There was an occasion when I was in my room in the nurses' home and I felt there was a weird presence around, though I couldn't explain why. I opened the door and there was a man standing right in the doorway with his face about six inches away from mine, at which point I slammed the door, pushed my bed up against it and heard him smashing the place up a bit before he left.

In those situations, you have only a split-second to decide what to do, but the main thing is to put something between you and them, whether it is distance by running, or by shutting a door on them, or picking up a chair. Whatever it is, you need to react quickly, and I know this is all a bit grim and horrible, but if women don't think about these things, they are not going to be prepared and they will suffer as a result.

One piece of advice I gave to my daughters, which I hated having to do, because it catapulted them out of innocence into a world of terrible possibilities, was, 'If anyone ever pulls up next to you in a van and asks you for some advice, or to come nearer, you must walk away from them.' A child at their school was walking past a van. She was probably eleven or twelve at the time and the driver said to her that he'd got a piece of carpet stuck in the van and he wasn't small enough to get in and pull it out. Would she crawl into the back of the van and get it out for him?

Thankfully, she was sensible enough not to accede to his request and she ran away and was fine. But there are many occasions when people are being friendly to you, particularly people who do not have the best intent and if you are not streetwise, you might easily say, well, all right, I'll help somebody out here.

The urge to be helpful that is drummed into all females is still powerful enough to override caution. When I was a nurse (and supposedly a streetwise adult) at one point, I drove my car into the car park quite late at night and a guy knocked on the windscreen. I was a bit naïve and trusting then . . . I thought he was going to ask me the way somewhere, so I wound the window down and he shoved his penis into my car, quite near my face. Of course, everybody said to me afterwards 'Why didn't you just wind the window up, and de-penis him?' But I didn't have electric windows, so I leaned on my car horn very loudly, someone rushed out of the nurses' home and he ran away.

If You Don't Like Something, Say So

It's just a case of trusting that instinct and acting on it, because a lot of us have an unerring need to be polite/not cause a fuss/not embarrass ourselves by misjudging the situation and we need to fight that.

This attitude is entirely responsible for the appalling crimes that went on during the seventies at the BBC and similar organisations. Absolutely everybody pretty much ignored what was happening and Savile and co. were allowed to run riot.

Primary school children are now taught a very straight-forward and direct way of stopping behaviour that they don't like: '*I don't like that because it makes me feel [sad/angry/scared]*'; but of course they need to tell another adult about it too. If the abuse is verbal they can say: '*In future could you not [talk to me/treat me] like that.*'

This gives me some hope for the future. After all, the people whose behaviour is making you feel unsafe might not necessarily recognise or care that that is what they are doing. It offers such a good approach to stopping any situation you're not happy with, not least because some-times the people trying to take advantage of you aren't strangers. (See 'How to Manage a Bully' and 'How Not to Fall in Love' for more on that.)

14

SOCIAL MEDIA IS NOT SOCIABLE

I liked a tweet this morning; it was from a blackbird in my garden.

I love Mumsnet because it is a rich tapestry of modern mothering with some hilarious blindsiders thrown in. In some ways the posts on Mumsnet are a bit like tabloid newspapers because they need to catch the eye for people to answer. My favourite section is Am I Being Unreasonable? or AIBU, where women (and men, though fewer) check a moral issue, inviting reaction. Even the premise makes me laugh. Some people's moral compasses are well out.

For example a woman suffering from depression recently only had one respondent whereas the highest scorer on the day I looked, with 373 posts, was about parking or something similar. Perhaps my favourite head-line to an AIBU in the last few days is 'People keep having sex in my hedge', which was very much enjoyed by the Mumsnetters. Mumsnet seems to be a real mix of middle-class professionals and ordinary working mums and SAHMs (stay-at-home ones) and it is brilliant for testing your thoughts about something out on a wider audience. Topics of great controversy recently have been Brexit and transgender issues, so it's not all just, 'My husband is an arse,' and 'I can't get my nets white.'

I would have loved Mumsnet to have been around when my children were small as so many tricky problems arise to do with sleeping, eating and what to do if they have a broad bean stuck up their nose and you get a really varied set of replies from people.

Everyone has a Mumsnet name and the best one I've come across is 'Eat Shit Derek'. I'd love to know the history behind that. I dip in occasionally if I feel moved to but mostly I just enjoy everyone else.

Social media is an important part of socialising and connection in the modern world. I use it. You use it. We all use it, but sometimes it is very hard not to see the online technology explosion of the last couple of decades as anything but pure evil, and forget it is merely another electronic conduit for the spreading of human malevolence. Of course, it spreads benevolence and does good things too, but it seems to me that it is human nature to major on the evil that humans do. So apart from charity pages, we tend to hear very little about online goodness, and an awful lot about online badness.

Let me ask a question. Who would not give up the ability to buy a book a little bit cheaper, if it shut down a paedophile group displaying online abuse? Or who would not forgo an online workout to stop the spread of live streaming of appalling murders? Clearly, those are two completely spurious questions, because we can't put this stuff back in Pandora's box, so we all have to learn to live with and develop coping strategies for it.

To a certain extent this is a knee-jerk reaction to a world that is pretty different to the world I grew up in, and maybe, although I don't want to admit it, I'm not seventeen any more and I'm very often put in the position of being sniggered at by my daughters when I use an old-fashioned word or get a modern word wrong. And it's what I used to do when my parents did the same thing, like my dad saying, 'This show's very trendy.' Hilarious. I rather like the continuity. Connections between children are really important and developing friendships teaches kids how to handle themselves in the world. Social media has completely changed the way children and teenagers learn to make friends and forge relationships and I find it unsettling at times. Obviously I'd like to stalk both my children on social media but when I really think about it, I'm not sure I would. Their private lives are their private lives and I would hope that if one of their friends was really concerned about them they would tell me.

Similarly, my parents had no idea what was going on, what different drugs really were or where I was and what I was doing. They had a good try at physically stalking me, but it was hardly ever successful and the only times I was found out were when my alibi was faulty or a friend blurted things out.

Another time, a friend and I bought some cigarettes for

asthmatics (yes, that is really true) as they had Benzedrine in them, and made some tea. We had two cups each, then I went home. Two hours later her mum was on the phone to my mum saying she'd tried to jump out of the window, totally blaming me – and it was her bloody idea.

Where we once all did whatever we did in person, hanging out at the bus stop after school or chatting on the phone, now everything is virtual. While there are some benefits to the change, they are far outweighed by the dangers of spending too much time online and becoming disconnected from the real world.

It is relentless too: the online world is always there and it's impossible to take a break from it. When I was a teenager I would have been horrified by the argument that returning to my stressful and boring family home and having a break from my friends was keeping me sane, but now I think it might well have been.

Know Your Enemies

Are there many parents out there still who don't have much of a clue how all the social media platforms work? Yes, me! So I had to ask my daughters and here's a rundown of everything you need to know.

FACEBOOK: only used by mums and dads; what a damning indictment of Facebook. No one really uses it. Everyone has it and uses it to stalk people. (Not in the true sense of the word, but if you see a picture of someone and want to find out more about them.)

TWITTER: not the main thing. Not as bad as Facebook.

SNAPCHAT: this is the one. Send pictures and messages. Everything disappears within twenty-four hours. You can save messages and add them to your story. I have no idea what the fuck this means.

YOUTUBE: not really a social media platform; shows vloggers and various bands or old TV series. Young people follow it mainly to watch YouTubers.

INSTAGRAM: everyone uses this. Loved by youth. Can have group chat.

My favourite phrase that one of my daughters came up with is 'Sliding into someone's DMs'. To me this means putting on my Doc Marten boots. To them – changing from public forum to the private direct messaging.

So What Is Going So Wrong?

The major problem is the lawlessness and lack of regulation of the internet and social media, which are complicated by concepts such as making money and lack of responsibility. Let's start with the age of participants in social media. First of all, they are supposed to be thirteen on Facebook, for example, and I think the age on some platforms is going to be put up to sixteen. Well, that's absolutely laughable, because I knew seven- and eight-year-olds who were on Facebook, and you only have to say that you are thirteen in order for you to sign up to them. Now I've told them how unfashionable it is they won't be going there any more.

It's a problem because the companies want as many as possible to sign up, yet the responsibility is left to the parents to check on their children and try to prevent them being on social media that they are not considered to be old enough for. The irony of this is that the vast majority of children know their way round a computer ten times better than their parents do, so anything their parents try security-wise can very easily be circumvented by the children.

Unless the barrage of protective laws we need are set up pronto, as parents, it will remain pointless to put blocks on things, which in my day was the equivalent of my mum and dad hiding the Sunday magazine at the top of the cupboard if it had some rude or violent pictures in it. Of course, my brothers and I knew exactly where it was, so as soon as my mum and dad were out in the garden, we would simply climb up there and get the magazine and have a look at whatever was in it.

I feel we need a different approach. We should be saying to our children that we know all this appalling stuff is available, and either force them to talk to us about it, or my preferred option would be to say, 'Let's watch it together.' Then see what happens when you and your child sit down to watch some very extreme porn online. I think that might put them off for life. I also think that putting embarrassing pictures on Instagram might be good fun – obviously you will need to find out passwords . . . I'm sure friends can be bribed. And of course it wouldn't last very long but would be worth it.

We need to have some way of tracing Twitter, Instagram and Facebook posts back to the source, much more easily than we can now. I also believe that the companies that provide the platforms display a complete lack of responsibility. I've said it before, but I do genuinely think it is all about money. If you make it too difficult for people, they might not invest in your lovely communication platform. The only way to scare these companies into making a commitment to improve things is to vote with your feet, but the vast majority of users are not going to do that, because they like using them. I would imagine huge financial penalties might work to persuade big companies to be more responsible, but as many of them aren't paying their tax, it's not going to be easy.

Educate the Technologically Illiterate

Scams. I receive endless attempted scams, as do many people, and the problem is that I know they're scams, you know they're scams, but vulnerable elderly people on the whole do not recognise them as such, and they are the ones who tend to get fleeced. It is essential to educate the technologically illiterate, and I include myself in that, to deal more effectively with online scamming.

I think the generation up from me, i.e. my mum, are also having a crack at social media, although they know slightly less (if that's possible) than my generation. My mum can send an email but wouldn't have a clue how to attach a photo to it, for example, and she is threatening to Skype us all, so I'm looking forward to that.

What Is Real

There is a nightmarish *1984* quality these days to news delivered on the internet: it's extremely hard in some cases to tell whether it is true or not. 'Fake news' as it's come to be known lives in that area with online scams and the doctoring of images which attempts to convince us that something is the truth when it's a lie. Is the truth an absolute though?

I'm aware I've posed a question that will make some people's heads explode, because surely the truth is the truth is the truth for ever and ever amen.

The problem is that the truth always includes an element of human observation and two people at the same event can report things totally differently. That is then interpreted by various newspapers in a value-laden way and hey presto the original bare information of the case has dribbled out of our grasp. On the whole most people are trusting and that's why it's easy to fool them. Just as we have a comedy US President, so the online news is starting to become like a sitcom and I think the reality of it is that people decide what they want to believe and reject what they don't want to believe. The sad thing, though, is that lots of people wanted to believe, for example, that the NHS genuinely would benefit from Brexit. It turned out to be bollocks and in some ways, if we knew how many people voted for Brexit on that basis, shouldn't we have a recount? The depressing thing about politics and news is that the cynics among us are not surprised by this. Of course people lie to further their own fortune/career/political views and the internet allows us to tell even more sophisticated lies. However, this is counter-balanced by the fact that everyone pretty much can film things on their phone to prove validity, which is again counter-balanced by other people saying those pieces of video are fake ... and so it goes on.

I am not going to dwell on selfies for very long except to say most people grow out of them thankfully. Let's face it, even I can look half decent with make-up on and the right lighting, so constantly striving for the perfect image of yourself is pointless, unless you plan to conduct a relationship with someone online and never meet them in person, and with some people that is a very good idea.

Online Dating

On the face of it, online dating sounds like a cattle market.

In my day: get pissed, go and try your luck with the least Neanderthal bloke in the pub and find out next day that he is a battle re-enactment fan.

Today: if you want to find someone who also loves museums and rollerblading and is actually looking for a relationship: well, no problem.

But some dating websites like Tinder are obsessed with looks. I would have been swiped left within microseconds.

Apart from that, one of the dangers of online dating sites is that you have to take people at their word. And there are sites where any man who wants to can roam untrammelled through endless female profiles without having to reveal his sexual history in any way, so is it better to risk it, knowing that there may be some dangerous people lurking, or go back to the traditional venue of friend's wedding, Sainsbury's or STD clinic? All right, not Sainsbury's.

As we know, a lot of vulnerable young women have been fooled into going to meet guys who have turned out to be not quite what they were hoping or expecting. This is playing on the rather naïve fantasies of these women and it won't be something that is sorted out until these guys' backgrounds are fully investigated. And that should likewise be the responsibility of the company that owns the website and is making a packet out of it.

Really the most important thing if you are meeting on a date arranged online is to DO IT IN PUBLIC. Do not agree to meet in a secluded spot in the middle of nowhere or go to the house of someone you've never met before. In some ways this advice is so obvious you can't believe it has to be constantly repeated. But it does: DO IT IN PUBLIC.

Sometimes online dates are a disaster as are real-life blind dates and you will want to bail pronto. Woman up and just tell them is my advice. You can do all the crawling out on all fours, climb out through the window, fake a text etc., etc., but really all you need is to say, 'Look I'm really sorry, this just isn't working out for me, can we call it to a halt?'

Unless the man is completely unreasonable he will understand. As someone who has been caught on all fours, semi-pissed, outside a pub toilet trying to crawl past a half door with glass in the top bit, to find my blind date staring down at me with a puzzled expression, I wish that's what I'd done rather than getting to my feet and legging it.

Learn from my humiliating experience and end all disastrous dates with a seamless, kindly, dignified exit.

Trolls and Bullying

Another issue that I have with social media is the easy anonymity, and therefore the unaccountability of the participants. So, in many cases you find men and sometimes paedophiles pretending to be children, or school bullies treating other kids in the most sadistic way online and getting away with it because their identity can't be traced.

Feminists have had a particularly rubbish time trying to deflect the charming messages sent to them by trolls. When Caroline Criado Perez had the nerve to suggest putting Jane Austen on a ten pound note, she received a barrage of terrifying rape and murder threats. When her two trolls were caught and taken to court, it transpired that they weren't bothered by having a woman on a banknote, they had kept going because they found the terror campaign and the notoriety exciting. And incidentally one of them was a young woman. What? I just cannot really take that in. I like to think of trolls as living in a barn together, coming up with nastier and nastier things to say to feminists and then firing them off, cackling as they do. But getting a message from a troll is far more frightening when that troll is anonymous. If you could see a picture of them and see what sort of life they live, nine times out of ten you would realise this was a person who was rather sad and disturbed, who's had a bit of a shit life so far, and that would make dealing with the appalling messages they are sending much easier.

In the olden days this kind of mean-spiritedness didn't get any further than angry neighbours writing poison pen letters about each other (they are normally written in green ink in a very scrawly, unsettling kind of way). The terrible thing about social media is that it gives this vitriol such a powerful platform. There's a real danger that the fear of this kind of bullying could stop women speaking out altogether. Women cannot allow this sort of threat to make them cower. Women have got to get arsey, be uncompromising and get lippy with it.

I think it's important to manage your time on social media a bit more fruitfully. My suggestion is that every time you have an urge to spend time on social media you eat a doughnut. The result of this is that you will become so fat and spotty you won't want to do selfies any more and will turn your attention towards weight loss classes. Well, I didn't say it would be a brilliant suggestion.

15

HAVING FUN

I ended up at some bloke's flat after a party. Got so drunk, found myself on the bus the next morning with carpet burns all over my chin – where he'd tried to drag me out of his flat.

My sixteenth birthday party was like every other teenage party has ever been – always slightly on the edge of out of control. My mum and dad had promised to come back late to give us a chance to really have fun. Then they broke their word and arrived back half an hour earlier than they had promised. By that time the party was in full swing and it was going like a dream: snogging couples lay around everywhere emboldened by cider, music blared out of the open window and the snacks distributed themselves unevenly across the carpet. I'm sure there was even the obligatory couple upstairs in my mum and dad's bedroom attempting full sexual intercourse

My friend Mouse (not her real name) opened the door and began the proceedings by throwing up on my dad's feet – not a great start . . .

This caused my dad to march into the house like a deranged bouncer shouting, 'Right, everyone out! The fun's over.' Little did he know that in my life the fun was just beginning.

There is some sort of unspecified biblical threat hovering around the idea of having fun, because many of us seem to have absorbed the belief that we will pay for our fun by being punished further down the line. Well, it's all a question of how you do your fun and what you use.

So fun-wise, let's look at the big five, at least in my opinion.

Alcohol

It is hard to believe that in the olden days, nobody went near water because it contained plagues of various hues. Can you imagine only drinking beer all the time instead of water? I know some of you are going 'yeah', but how horrible would that sticky-gum, hangover gloop at the top of your mouth be, if you had it every day.

Without going into too much scientific detail let's talk about how alcohol affects the brain; the common effects are:

Slows you down, i.e. slurred speech.
Your behaviour becomes disinhibited.
You feel happier, or if you're sad – sadder.
Wanting to have sex.
Being crap at it.

What happens here is that alcohol affects the performance of neurotransmitters that control brain activity. And really, if you want to know more than this, read a science book. Let's just say we all know what it's like to be sober, half pissed and completely out of it and I don't want to hold you up by throwing lots of big words at you (like I understand them).

Used in moderation (that completely hideous word thrown at people the world over by GPs who seriously can't believe that that is going to have any effect whatsoever), many people drink alcohol to manage their social anxiety, which many of us have if we are catapulted into a room of strangers; not literally of course, because if I was that would cause serious injury to many. While we're on the subject, said the pedant, may I try to arrest the march of the 'Literally' brigade.

I heard someone say recently, 'I literally died.' This sort of hyperbole has been sanctioned recently by those wot know good language but if you're thinking of using 'literally' just substitute the word 'actually' and you'll know if you're about to say something ridiculous.

Pardon that meander into snobbery, but as I said alcohol is used by people to calm themselves down if they're anxious; not a good idea just before your driving test, by the way.

This works okay if you do it in moderation but can get out of hand if you need to do it all the time.

One drink takes the edge off your worries.
Two drinks, three drinks, four drinks: getting slightly gobby, not yet slurring.

Ten drinks: will sleep with someone you've just met; you are pissed, vulnerable and friends shouldn't leave you to cope on your own.

Let's not be too down on alcohol: it's great for oiling the wheels at parties, for celebrations, for lowering inhibitions if that's what you want, and try and imagine a party without alcohol. Hmm. Also, if you want to chat someone up but your butterflies and dry mouth won't let you, it can be a real help; and if you're rejected then some more can enable you to do quite spectacular rants to your friends.

In my teenage years, I drank a fair amount. I was in and out of the pubs of Hastings from a fairly young age, pursued not by a bear, but by my mum and dad. We did a pretty good impression of a 1930s black and white comedy, because they would appear at one door as I left by the other, and they never did catch me in the vicinity of the pub. Even though they knew I was there, and were very frustrated by the fact, it was always back at home that we would meet up again.

In those days, the sorts of drinks that were aimed at women, and attractive because they tasted very sweet, were vodka and lime, which everyone loved and which was a bit like drinking lime-flavoured phlegm, not very nice really; Babycham, which was a tiny little bottle of pretend champagne with a deer on it, that was very cheap; or a Snowball, which was Advocaat and sparkling lemonade, with a dash of lime juice, and they put a glacé cherry in it with a cocktail stick. Yuck! None of those particularly appealed to me. I was a lager drinker and I loved bottles of pils, because they were quite strong and you didn't have to buy too many to get absolutely rat-arsed.

I have a strange relationship with alcohol. My mum gets pissed on half a teaspoon of sherry and my tolerance is similar. I don't really drink at all now because the hangovers are monumental and I associate drinking with getting absolutely wasted and behaving badly and now I have kids, I don't feel that's a brilliant example to set.

Besides, hangover cures are never that brilliant. I recommend a full English, a pint of orange juice, two cans of Coke and some apple crumble, but that's just 'cause I like all those.

My favourite drinks are lager, Brandy Alexander, champagne and Baileys-type drinks – like having an alcoholic milkshake. However, I did really go to town once with something called Royal Chocolate Mint Liqueur when I lived in the nurses' home and ended up throwing it all up down the side of the bed like a plank and went back to sleep; so undignified and not the behaviour of a lady.

Drinking games are popular if you want to have your liver removed the next day. There is a drinking game to cap all drinking games in which you have to drink everything the characters drink in the film *Withnail and I* as you watch it. No, I haven't. Rumour has it that if you did you would die, but I've never tested that out.

Over the years, everyone becomes aware of the person in their group who doesn't buy their round. It's such a cliché. I favour an anonymous note.

If you realise you're really pissed and you don't want to be, stop drinking and go home, or have a black coffee or go for a run. Yep, good luck with that last one.

The relaxed attitude towards drink of the baby-boomers, of whom I am one, has definitely coloured the attitude of adolescent humans today, because from what I understand, many of them in their late teens and twenties are giving up alcohol altogether. Possibly rightly so, as it can do an awful lot of damage to livers, and immense harm to relationships and so many other aspects of human life that you already know about, so I won't go into them.

Of course, people have always loved drinking, because it enables them to behave extremely badly and then say, 'Oh, I was drunk, so the alcohol was responsible and not me.' I used to find that a very useful excuse when I was younger and woke up in a field without any shoes.

When I was growing up, the progress towards adulthood seemed to be that you go totally mad with alcohol when you're about fifteen, and then your mum finds you face down in your bedroom, next to a puddle of something unidentifiable, and berates you solidly for an hour and then you go out and do it again the next night. Alcohol can be dangerous for young people whose 'I've had too much' area of the brain is switched off and they end up taking an overdose, which is not how people often describe it, but there are numbers of teenagers who die from excessive alcohol imbibed during drinking competitions or parties, which seems so tragic and points towards friends just having to be more vigilant.

As you move towards adulthood and become more mature, you cut down on alcohol and are a bit more grown up, and by the time you get to forty, most people are hardly drinking at all, because they can't look after children properly with hangovers. I'm giving you the idealised version here. Or else they have become dependent upon alcohol and will struggle for the rest of their lives, unless they can find a way to deal with it, and unfortunately the only real answer to the question, How can I stop my alcohol addiction? is abstinence. Terrible for people who love drinking. I feel for them. Then of course there is the Wine O'Clock Brigade, hordes of middle-class people who have far more than the recommended level of alcohol and are just round the corner from alcoholism. It's a lottery, guys, and who wants to live to a hundred anyway?

But that acute side of the alcohol problem is not one that is spoken about very much, because the perception is that it happens to relatively few people. The problem with alcohol is that it is knitted in to the fabric of society and ever present at gatherings, sporting events (many fans carry it in inside them if there is an alcohol ban), festivals, corporate events, you name it; probably the only place alcohol is not to be seen is primary school sports days.

Cigarettes

I used to smoke – and oh, the joy! Little tubes of delight, the writer Dennis Potter used to call them, puffing away on them right until the very last. I started smoking on the school bus, as did quite a few of my friends. I was on the school bus for two and a half hours each way every day in the week, so it was a bit boring and we didn't have much else to do. Then once I left home at sixteen my smoking rocketed because I liked it, and I didn't really think about stopping until I got into my mid to late thirties, by which time I had smoked one hell of a lot of fags. But I did give up in my late thirties because I wanted to have children, and I didn't want to puff my way through a pregnancy, and then blow smoke into the pram.

So I stopped. I had a little blip, four or five years down the line, when I started again very briefly, because someone offered me one at a party and I had no willpower at all. But I do not smoke now. All right, that's not strictly true. I occasionally have one if there's a group of people at whatever work I'm doing, outside, huddling round glowing fag ends, and I get tempted.

The thing about cigarettes is that they help people to control their anxiety. Cigarettes are great for people who need to suppress their appetite, like ballet dancers – the ones I've met smoke like there is no tomorrow. Sorry, I sound like I hang around with ballet dancers. I don't! – But fags are a social lubricant, and people in groups use them at parties, because they have something in common – being social lepers. There's even been a word coined to describe smoking and flirting: 'smirting'. Terrible word but a very enjoyable thing to do, until you get to kiss the ashtray next to you. Nothing beats feeling like a woman of mystery hanging around outside a pub, cigarette in hand, while drunkenly talking to someone attractive (however much you might have really looked like a failed extra from *Coronation Street* instead). So not only are you viewing a potential beau through clouds of smoke, but you've probably had a drink or two and put your beer goggles on. For those of us who are less than beautiful beer goggles are a godsend. A wild night spent goggled up (but more importantly my potential partner's got a very thick pair on), with a packet of fags has been enjoyed very much by me on several occasions.

Cigarettes are also useful as a weapon. I was on the receiving end of this in Edinburgh once, when a very angry Scots woman, who didn't like me for some reason and I never found out why, stubbed her fag out on my arm. I can attest to the fact that they do hurt if you grind them into someone's body.

If you want to keep smoking for your whole life, you need to be a gambler. Most people don't want to gamble and they give up some time. You can give up in many ways; there are lots of things to help, patches, chewing gum and sweets. I used sweets and I cut down over three weeks or so until on the final day I had one in the morning and one in the evening. It was crap, I was irritable, frustrated and getting through forty packets of Murray Mints an hour. Vaping wasn't an option at the time or I would probably have had a crack at that, although I don't think they do a rhubarb crumble one, so maybe not. Who knows whether I gave up early enough in my late thirties not to do any damage? I'll let you know.

DRUGS

Right, drugs. I've had a few, but then again, too few to mention. That's not quite true, I've actually tried every-thing – that is, all the drugs that were around in my day.

Is that laudanum? I hear you ask. No, it isn't. It is cannabis, amphetamines, LSD, heroin: I had a little go at everything. Here's a quick rundown.

Cannabis

Cannabis has always been described as a 'gateway' drug, i.e. something that leads you through to trying more harmful drugs. I'm not sure I subscribe to that. I know many people who tried cannabis, coughed a lot and then never tried anything else. I read a study when I was at university that suggested that we need to learn how to experience the effects of cannabis, almost be taught it, and I think the more experienced dope smoker in the corner does set up an informal seminar when novices appear in terms of how you should approach the process of getting stoned.

In my day, there were rituals involved in rolling joints and if you did a bad one everyone would laugh at you. You needed three joints to get over it.

I'm not going to go into details about the chemical reaction in your brain. Suffice to say:

Makes you hungry.
Makes you laugh.
Makes you relax.

I quite liked cannabis although I wouldn't have bothered if someone else hadn't managed it all. I was the cannabis equivalent of the person who always smokes everyone else's cigarettes.

Added to that, cannabis has been much in the press lately

as a drug to treat a variety of conditions from epilepsy to MS. Surely it can't be long before it is legalised.

Amphetamines (and Cocaine)

Amphetamines basically speed you up. They are also used in the medical profession although not quite so much these days. In fact many of the drugs used to treat children with hyperactivity disorders are based on amphetamines which is completely counter-intuitive and you have to catch the little buggers first.

Because amphetamines suppress your appetite and speed you up a bit, they were inevitably used for weight loss, unfortunately being pretty addictive too so not a great success overall.

So the effects of amphetamines:

Feeling euphoric mood-wise.
Suppression of hunger.
Energy.
Keeps you active for longer.
Can cause psychosis.

Amphetamine psychosis is a well-known condition and happens to individuals who are in some way vulnerable to it. When I worked in mental health A&E, a very well-known singer was brought in by the police having taken too much speed, but the Hippocratic Oath prevents me from telling you who it was.

Cocaine has pretty similar effects to amphetamines and is the party drug of choice for many bands, entertainers, City boys and those who can afford it.

It is administered nasally through a rolled-up tenner or similar or, according to legend, literally blown up the arse of various musicians and actors as it is absorbed more quickly via this route. Overuse results in these bits being worn away and for years there was a rumour going round about a famous actress that she'd had so much cocaine anally administered she had to have that area replaced. How on earth that works, God only knows.

The effects of cocaine:

Increased confidence.
Sleeplessness.

There is a right old come-down with coke known as 'the three-day grumps', although obviously some people who take drugs are naturally grumpy so it's difficult to tell.

LSD

LSD is a drug that really alters your perception of reality so visual hallucinations are a big feature of it. I tried this with a friend when I was probably about fourteen or fifteen. What a brilliant night I had. I spent some time conversing with a poster of Bob Dylan on the wall and then later just staring at a plate of ham sandwiches, all of which had the face of Andy Williams (Google it!). The walls visibly breathed and the trees looked so magnificent that I thought at the time I would start up a tree appreciation society.

This happy memory was leavened by having the opposite experience some years later when someone spiked my drink in a pub. Walking home I passed a phone box that had a monk swinging a dead cat in it, then a bright pink coach, ablaze with lights, mounted the pavement and tried to run me over. I jumped into a garden that appeared to have a huge pack of tethered wolves with dripping jaws. By now I was shit-scared. I knew intuitively that it was something druggy. I ran to my brother's flat and he poured orange juice down me for the whole night and in the morning I was fine.

The joy and fun of LSD are therefore undercut by the risks people take because they are so far removed from reality and tragic accidents can happen. Again, if every one of your friends is doing it, no one is going to be sensible enough to keep an eye on everyone.

Heroin

My first proper boyfriend was a heroin addict, but it took me a while to realise this. He was very posh, and had a riot of curly hair and an elfin face, a very popular look in the days of T. Rex.

To his credit, he didn't try to lure me into his evil habit; he never used it in front of me. And the thing to bear in mind about opiates is that they are, on the whole, reasonably safe if their administration is controlled. It is the dirty needles and infections that do a lot of damage. On the outpatients drug unit where I worked we had a group of heroin addicts in their sixties who had come over from Canada in the early 1960s, attracted by the liberal drug laws, and were still going strong on a cocktail of pure heroin and clean drug paraphernalia.

I have always felt that heroin, far from being a party drug, is used by long-term addicts to fill a huge gap within themselves. Then their whole life becomes about getting that drug, with a concomitant drop in moral principles as many people will commit the most appalling crimes to get their next dose.

I didn't try heroin until I was in my twenties and in fact I did what is known as 'chasing the dragon' for a few weeks. It didn't do a huge amount for me, thank God, or I probably wouldn't be here telling you about this. The overriding effect is an overwhelming feeling of wellbeing that causes all your troubles physical and mental to recede into the background. Sounds amazing, doesn't it? And that is the problem. I wouldn't even try it if I were you . . . just in case.

Dealing with Addiction

I feel there is such a thing as an addictive personality, which one day we will be able to genetically map. Until that time teenagers will experiment recklessly with drugs and the unlucky ones will fall by the wayside. It is the group whose lives are full of pain physically or mentally who are at the mercy of drugs. Sorry, folks, not very funny, is it?

Every generation have their own drug stories to tell. I'm just telling you about the ones I experienced, some of which of course remain popular today. But I suppose I'm relieved to say Es, skunk and legal highs have passed me by. Probably just as well. I'm sure I've had enough excitement in that department.

But for God's sake, legalise cannabis. I have a really good friend with MS, and God knows she could do without being a fugitive from the law.

Food

The next fun pastime is food. I've had far too much fun with food over the years, as you can probably tell by looking at me. I place the blame squarely on carbs and genes. I lost about three stone as a teenager but I didn't like the way various people treated me; didn't really like that predatory thing that some men do when they fancy you and so I never tried too hard after that. My top ten list of foods includes toast, French bread, potatoes, pasta ... hmm, there seems to be a pattern developing there. I actually do really like vegetables and salad but not on their own and it seems that now I am sixty if I eat more than 7 calories a day, I put on weight. I think that's because I was brought up on a very traditional diet for the 1960s, which involved a lot of the previous. Funnily enough I was never very keen on cakes – not to the point where I wouldn't eat them though, but the plainer the cake the better as far as I'm concerned. When I first started doing stand-up I did lots of jokes about cakes because of what I felt was the incongruity of a fat person in our judgemental society liking them, given that most big people do not proudly exclaim 'I like cakes' because they are too embarrassed. Cake references have followed me around ever since. My favourite cake is either a Victoria sponge or a doughnut and most other cakes don't really do it for me.

In fifty years' time, fat people will potentially be able to take a tablet and not be fat any more. Grrrrr. That will be a hundred years too late. The answer to being overweight can be condensed, I'm afraid, into a very small sentence. You can try all different types of diet or measure your metabolism, you can stand on a plate that wobbles, you can do so many things, but it all comes down – particularly if you are the same age as me – to one thing. Eat hardly anything.

You can improve this by doing exercise. Eating very little is bloody miserable, and doing exercise can cheer you up a bit, because it releases endorphins into your bloodstream, but that makes you hungry too. Bloody typical.

Sex

One other fun pastime that many of us attempt from about the age of sixteen until roughly the menopause if you are a woman – maybe beyond – is, of course, sex.

If I am comparing attitudes to sex now with when I was a teenager, some things are similar and some are very different. Let's start with the similarities.

As a nation I think we find it difficult to talk about sex, which is why British comedy has majored in innuendo, as far as sex is concerned, for many years. And that always allowed us to swerve round talking about sex honestly. There are so many things you can say if you use a euphemism about sex that are simply too much for most of us to manage in plain English.

In the fifties when I was born I don't think anyone ever mentioned anything to do with sex because it was too embarrassing and so seaside postcards had to do the job. When sex exploded in the sixties I think a handful of daring women embraced it but it took a while for the rest of the population to get round to it. In our heads, sex is so tied up with sin and not supposed to be a pleasure that I think many people found it difficult to contemplate without some sort of help (see alcohol). And I think to some, shyness about sex still exists and, for example, asking someone to wear a condom is a bridge too far. Pornography was not available in my day to my teenage self and now you can't get away from it online apparently.

It seems highly likely that teenage boys watching porn will believe that is how sex should be, when we all know the reality is much more fumbly and short-lived, particularly when you are a teenager. My advice on sex is probably boringly predictable . . .

Lower your expectations.

Sex in films is ridiculously portrayed from porny writing and screaming to misty-eyed tender encounters that look nothing like sex. Also, some individuals are a better fit sexually than others. I once stayed with a partner for far too long because he was very good at sex, but a very annoying person.

Try and talk about sex without sounding like rude *Blind Date* and take a break if you're getting too embarrassed. Try things, have fun, but remember if something feels wrong and you want it to stop say so.

And don't send pictures of all your bits to your current boyfriend because in six months' time the year 10 football team could all be looking at them.

Now we are back to the biblical again. Religions have a huge amount to say about when we can do it and who we do it with. Take HIV/AIDS, for example, which was designated by some people as a punishment from above for gay men daring to have sex with each other. In the 1980s even the ads warning people about AIDS looked like the tablets that God had left lying around on the mountain for Moses to see. A kind of glowering punishment theme going on there.

The fact of the matter is, if you get a disease like AIDS it is not a biblical judgement, it is just very bad luck and it means that you didn't take enough precautions. Syphilis, gonorrhoea, herpes, chlamydia – they all fall into the category of things you can get if your partner doesn't wear a condom, and you have to, have to, have to, if you possibly can. If you don't care about catching a disease, fine, don't read this next bit, but if you can, ignore the pleas about it being a much lovelier experience for them. Simply return the favour by saying, 'A lovelier, brief experience for you may result in a much less lovelier, possibly lifetime experience for me. So, no.'

We are told we can experience all the fun things I have mentioned. There is nothing integrally evil about them, depending on who you talk to, but we are advised to do everything in moderation. To me, that is quite depressing, and I took the route that is very different from moderation, of doing it a lot, and then not doing it any more. Moderation is the murderer of fun.

Later in life, sex is less important – to women, it seems, although yes, some still like it, but more ancient old geezers still want to go at it like trains.

So what do I do for fun now?

I like gardening, knitting and running a brothel.

16

NOT HAVING FUN

I used to live with a guy who always used to strum his guitar endlessly, or Exhibit A as I used to call it.

So what do you do when it all goes wrong? We all have difficult times, but this chapter is not about trying to avoid these things happening, because they inevitably will, it is more how you deal with them when they do.

Here I want to tackle some areas of life where when it goes wrong it can feel really overwhelming – particularly when you are surrounded, as you so often are, by people who seem to be handling things so much better than you. The fact is at any one time a lot of people are struggling with something and you just don't know about it because they are hiding it, but there are coping strategies available to us all – no, not getting pissed all the time, madam.

Live to Work or Work to Live?

Let's start with work, because unless you are really lucky, it is a part of life that can be really stressful at one time or another. Confucius said, 'Find a job you love and you'll never work another day in your life.' Obviously he had a lovely job just saying things in short-form sentences, like an ancient Tweeter.

Sadly the employment market doesn't really offer the right proportion of jobs that most people would like to do: huge-salary-for-doing-bugger-all-type jobs.

The search for the truly satisfying job goes on and in the meantime we all have to eat and pay rent/mortgage or whatever your arrangement is. In a lot of ways, work is like a grown-up version of school, with all the same types of people, so there is the bully, the annoying person, the skiving person and the aggressive person. They are all there, except now you are an adult, of course, you are expected to deal with them in an adult way.

But some people simply can't, because when things go wrong, it takes them back to when they were at school. How many times do you read in the paper or online that someone has been signed off work with stress? And how few times do you know exactly what that entails, because it is one of those blanket phrases that covers a myriad of different possibilities. It is important to deal with these problems before they get really bad.

I've had some stressful times at work and one that comes to mind – and this is pathetic, but it was a very long time ago and I was about seventeen – was when I worked for a very 'difficult' French chef (has there ever been a chef who was easy to work for? I wonder). I was in the kitchen doing everything except what he did, which was the cooking, I suppose. He was extremely aggressive and sarcastic, and over the months that I worked there, working very hard and very long hours at weekends, I never got anything positive from him.

One day he walked past a massive bowl of garlic that I had just peeled and prepared and accidentally knocked it on to the floor. He didn't say, 'Oh sorry, that's really clumsy of me,' or 'Let me pick it up.' He just looked at me and went, 'Pick it up.' I'd had enough by then, so I picked it all up and once I had popped the last bulb of garlic on top of the pile in the bowl, I emptied it out all over the floor again and said, 'Pick it up yourself,' and walked out.

It wasn't exactly sensible and I wouldn't recommend it to everyone, but I could afford to lose that job as it was only part-time – and if you need to keep a job, you can't behave like that – but it felt bloody great and it gave me so much satisfaction. Because there are far too many people like that guy who go through their lives treating everyone like shit, and it gets to a point where everybody is too afraid to say anything, particularly if he/she is the boss. And the worst thing is that because no one speaks up the bully assumes that this sort of behaviour is acceptable and continues to do it. These bullies, especially if they are the boss, have so much control over your emotional wellbeing at work, so if you can possibly afford to leave and find another position, then you absolutely should do it. But a lot of people can't. They are stuck in jobs that they absolutely hate. They are on zero-hours contracts, their tips taken away from them to swell the boss's coffers and options to change job and get something better are pretty limited.

In this case, you need to work out a strategy for how to deal with this stressful situation without damaging yourself too much emotionally, because obviously the fallout from working with someone sadistic is incredibly undermining and depressing. The first thing, perhaps, is to do your utmost not to take it personally. Start from the standpoint of knowing that they are a horrible person and they are never going to change, but you are a decent person, and use everything you can in your power or imagination to steer clear of them at work.

People are often far too polite and they let situations go on for too long, and then they explode. So that's another thing: intervene sooner and try to do something about it. Maybe transfer yourself to a different department, or get a few people on board for support, and realise that you are not the problem, but as a grown-up you have worked out a way to deal with it. If there's any way to detach yourself from their behaviour enough to see it as funny, rather than frightening, it would really help. I'm not necessarily suggesting you laugh hysterically the next time the boss comes along with another unreasonable demand, but there are some possibilities.

So what can you do?

Well, first I would try your hardest not to ever be on your own with your boss. This has two functions. First, bullies find it easier to bully without an audience, so hopefully they'll go easier on you. Second, their bullying will be witnessed by others, so should you decide to take any action it will not just be your word against theirs.

The Root of All Evil?

I now come to the delightful topic of money. On the whole, we are absolutely enchanted by money, and it makes some people who haven't got any commit criminal acts to get some. It also makes people who have got loads of money commit criminal acts to make even more, or to hang on to what they have got. If you've got no money, there is nothing worse in many ways. I know everyone thinks I live in a castle and I'm loaded, and I am not going to deny that I have made enough money to be very comfortable. But that doesn't mean to say that I didn't once have money worries, because as a student nurse I earned very little compared to a lot of people.

So I know what it's like having to make difficult decisions about debt priorities. As a student nurse it was pretty much a hand-to-mouth existence and always an anxious time standing in front of the cashpoint towards the end of the month in case it wouldn't give me any money (still feel like that!). That time makes me appreciate having money now, and it makes me also feel sorry for people who haven't got any. But I don't believe many people who are wealthy feel sorry for people who have no money; they prefer to think of them as scroungers and therefore they don't have to do anything about it or feel bad even though a lot of them profess to be Christians.

Saying that money isn't everything is usually said by people who have got money. If you haven't got any money, it is everything, of course it is. But with my background, I was raised to embody the Protestant work ethic. I was brought up to work always and I would have done any job to earn money. Some people think, I'm going to hold out until I've got a nice job, but if you really want to earn money you can't do that. You have to do anything that's going and I think quite a lot of people are just not prepared to do that. I have been a cleaner in a TB hospital, done hop-picking, working from six in the morning till seven at night, and worked in a truckers' pub in Uxbridge (yum), so I do know what it can be like.

And if you're thinking, Truckers' pub ... that bad? I once got pulled over the bar by a trucker and catapulted into his mountainous stomach, which was covered with a tattoo of a naked woman with her legs open, so he could canvass my opinion on its artistic merits.

I was neutral.

I feel like I am preaching here. I don't mean to, but what I would say is, I would like people with money to have a bit more sympathy towards people who haven't got any (money, not sympathy), and I probably include myself in that.

Beware of What You Wish For

Babies are another area of life where your fun can be seriously curtailed, because you have absolute freedom to do virtually what you want before you have babies. Then they come along and everyone thinks, I'm going to sling my baby on my back and walk round the world with my flip-flops on. Nothing's going to change. Sadly you're not going to do that, because babies need routine and you can't just take them wherever you are going and prop them up on the bar while you get pissed. They need that routine and you have got to provide it. Also, lovely as they are, and as wonderful as everyone tells you that it is, one of the biggest secrets in life is how hard it is to look after babies, and nobody tells you that until you've joined the club of worn-out, resentful, half-awake baby carers. That's why everyone with children tells you to get sleep, go to films, read, have luxurious showers, because these and other leisure pursuits fall away faster than you can say 'colic'.

The first thing to say is that it is bloody difficult to do it on your own. The second thing to say is that it is bloody difficult to do it if you have a partner. Your life is filled with crying and screaming. You crying, your partner screaming as you both compile venomous time sheets in your heads about who's done the most with which to judge and accuse your dearest love. You for feeling there has been an unfair division of labour, them feeling nagged, shouted at, ridiculed, humiliated, belittled, helpless, useless, confused . . . insert your own adjectives here.

If you have family and friends who want to help – lucky you.

You have also got to forget the myth about how wonderful it is all supposed to be. Although it is a bloody hard slog at times, in the end it pays off.

Third, follow your intuition. There's a whole industry of baby-raising books with all kinds of extreme and contradictory advice, but most people instinctively look after their babies with common sense, such as letting them go to sleep rather than taking them to a funfair at eleven o'clock at night, for example. Breastfeeding doesn't work for everyone but it is treated as a very shameful failure when it doesn't. If you're worried about anything, don't suffer in silence – ask for help. There is a whole support network out there created for exactly this. Ask your mum, doctor, health visitor, NCT mates, friend ... Babies are hard work, so don't feel you're a crap parent if you are not coping; try and involve other people in the care so you can get some sleep or have a shower – that's another thing, you never get a chance to have a proper wash. So you should bear that in mind: all parents are tired, all parents are resentful, all parents are angry and all parents are a bit smelly.

Let's Stick Together?

Like having children, there are many good things to marriage and long-term relationships, like having someone to go and buy you haemorrhoid cream so you don't have to announce it to the queue in the chemist in your best actor voice, with maximum projection, as the pharmacist seems to have forgotten his ear trumpet. But there's a reason that one in two marriages currently end in divorce. It's not easy maintaining a long-term relationship as that little devil 'Familiarity' is busy breeding contempt, because we all change, we bore, irritate and frustrate our partners and what we were looking for changes too.

Some of you may have noticed that I rather relentlessly slag off my husband in my stand-up set and I am often asked by people what he makes of it. Well, what he makes of it is that it's a comedy set and I think if the sorts of things comics say about their partners to rooms full of people were 100 per cent true, very few comedy marriages would survive.

My advice for your marriage is not very helpful, but you will know that when/if the moment comes to go, you will definitely recognise it. You don't need me to tell you. Incidentally this is discussed ad infinitum on Mumsnet so if you want some support in pinpointing if his last bad act was bad enough for you to split, run that past the Mumsnetters; they won't hold back.

My advice, for what it's worth (about 12p), is:

1. Don't have an affair.
2. Try and be nice to each other and if you can't, one of you has to go out.
3. Don't scream your heads off at each other in front of the kids.

I can't really think of anything else. It's nice if you have some things in common but not essential and if you are one of those women married to a man who is constantly on the lookout for other women, leave – unless you are constantly on the lookout for other men.

Always remember: the first rule of lifesaving is save yourself.

Get Well Soon . . .

When someone says, 'Oh, at least I've got my health,' people often think, Please shut up, what does that really mean? That phrase is something that a lot of us find hard to deal with, because we don't have much imagination. So if you are used to treating your health in a cavalier fashion and suddenly you are struck down with something, it can come as a huge shock how much it curtails certain aspects of your life.

Sometimes people say, 'I wish I had appreciated being healthy before I got ill,' and fair enough, that is a reasonable comment to make, but once you are ill what's the point of thinking you should have appreciated it?

We all go a bit bonkers when we are young – a lot of people smoke, drink and take drugs – but once you get older and start to grow up, try not to do excessive things, like drinking more than you should. It is hard to imagine the future – to jump forward thirty or forty years – and think, How might I be if I have my forty-second fag of the day now? That's impossible, but I'm telling you: how you might be is not good at all.

One of the things that people who like enjoying themselves say about giving up smoking is that it doesn't extend your life, it only feels like it. It does extend your life if you give up smoking, but then again, I can admire and understand the people who don't give up smoking and don't care whether their life is a bit shorter, particularly given the way that care for the elderly is organised at the moment. There is probably a whole raft of old people stuck in beds, miserable as sin, whose families don't come to see them, who think, I wish I'd smoked eighty fags a day, then I wouldn't even have to be here and put up with this crap.

I'm not trying to be mean here, I am only trying to look at life in a different way. What is the point of being fit and healthy if you are not prepared for an old age when you are stuck somewhere you don't want to be, and being patronised by a load of nurses? I can't understand that at all.

The End of the Road

Last on my list is death. I know that's not very cheerful, but because death is still such a taboo we tend not to think about it until it is accelerating down the road quite fast at us. Certain communities and cultures have a much better attitude towards death than we do. And we can learn from them. In our culture anything to do with death is immediately shelved, or shoved under the carpet, and even bereaved people find it difficult to know how to approach grieving. They do what most of us do, which is to put it to one side in their head and deal with it later.

It is so vital to talk to other people about it. I am writing this for myself as well as for you. My brother died three years ago and, to be honest, I have still not dealt with it properly. He lived in Germany with his family and he had stomach cancer. He died while I was on tour and I had to postpone some dates. I had one week off a TV series I was doing and that was it. The thing is that as a comic and someone who is recognisable as such, I pretty much still had to Carry On (as it sometimes seemed farcical) Regardless. I didn't really talk to anyone and filed it to Back of Mind to deal with at a later date. Not sure I have.

So in this instance, don't do what I did.

Five Unexpected Things About Someone Close to You Dying

1. That you don't believe it for ages.
2. That it makes you very, very, very angry.
3. It makes you want to change the shit bits in your life.
4. It made me not want to talk to anyone about it.
5. It made me wish other people were dead instead of my brother.

I think there are a lot of people who file death away because they feel embarrassed about expressing emotions or they actually can't face dealing with it – whatever that means, I still don't know. It is something that we all need to think about and get our head round. That doesn't mean that if you think about death it is actually going to happen, because we can all be quite superstitious as well.

So, read about it, explore the idea. It's going to happen to all of us – rich, poor, fat, thin, it doesn't matter – and it is coming down the line at you at some point. Think a little bit as you get older about how it is going to be for you and what you want, set up some rules and talk to your family about it. They will probably shut you up, because they are like you, but have a go at considering it.

17

PARENTING: THE GREAT CONSPIRACY

I suggested to my daughter the other day that she sent an email to her friend. She shook her head. 'Why not?' 'Because, Mum, I'm not a hundred years old.' That told me.

Most families these days tend to live far away from their relatives, but in the olden days, when I was a young'un, they would have been geographically close to both sets of grandparents, as well as their aunts, uncles and cousins. Nowadays that sort of support has been replaced by whatever you can find online: electronic parenting advice, or parenting communities like Mumsnet. In between the extended family giving you advice and all the online stuff, there are books, of course, but it was always very difficult to know which book on parenting to choose. Some of them were virtually fascist manuals on how to fuck up a child, while others were more like 'put them in the garden with some bunny rabbits', so when you were trawling through a bookshop it was impossible to tell which was going to be the right one for you.

In the long run, though, it doesn't matter whether you read *Five Languages by Five* or *Let the Little Buggers Get on With It*, the type of parent you are going to be is dormant and ready to go in a box marked, 'Genes and Own Family Dynamics'.

I came across a phrase a few years ago that chilled me to the bone. I paraphrase: 'The major element in the life of a child is the unlived life of the parent.' Yeah, sit back and think about that. It is so telling in the lives of many children. Bear in mind all those Neanderthal dads at football screaming at their kids in the hope that their 'advice' will result in a Premiership apprenticeship and abusing everyone who questions their language. I return to Mumsnet briefly to describe an incident in which a mother asked the guy next to her to keep the swearing down and received the very grown-up answer, 'Shut up, baggy tits.' When she grumpily remonstrated he followed up by calling her 'Jo Brand'. Not sure if I am a cipher for baggy tits or bad temper. Both presumably.

In my own case, my mother could have gone to Oxford but chose not to, which may explain why she was so keen for me, her only daughter, to do precisely that. I ended up going to Brunel.

As a child, you will quickly recognise what your parents want for you, acknowledge it and then decide what you want for yourself.

In upper-class and upper-middle-class families, there is still the attitude of a family firm. Many parents who are

GPs will produce little baby GPs, and lawyers will produce lawyers. These people flog their kids, obviously not literally, but they push their kids into doing what they consider to be a family tradition, and woe betide the poor child if they want to be a make-up artist or work at Bobby's Biscuits in Hereford. So my first bit of advice if you are going to be a parent is to think long and hard about your life up until this point and think to yourself, Are you determined to make your poor child scramble halfway up Everest, all because you wanted to and you never made it? And if so, stop right there.

At the other end of the parenting spectrum, the approach of most people I come across seems rather to be about trying to bring up their children in the opposite way to how they were brought up. We feel that we were damaged somehow and need to mitigate it in any way that we can. For example, because my parents were extremely strict when I was a teenager, I have a tendency to be rather too liberal, and I think that pattern is being repeated all over the country. This obviously implies that my children may grow up to be disciplinarians and so the wheel of inevitability turns again. I knew someone who was perhaps one of the most chaotic women I'd ever met, enjoying life, late nights, thoroughly irresponsible. Her child, however, was a nuclear version of Saffy from *Ab Fab*, beautifully and conservatively turned out, constantly cleaning and always cooking. I'm hoping that as I am a shit cook, one of my daughters will be brilliant and feed me as I sit lolling in my bath chair.

We are all carrying a template in our heads from the way we were brought up that, most of the time, we are not even aware of. You may look at yourself and think, Why am I doing this or Why am I reacting like that? Sometimes it is hard to uncover your motives for doing things, unless a therapist digs it up for you, and, let's face it, a lot of people either can't afford that or don't want to dig anything up. One example from my own life is that my father suffered from depression and I became a comedian. Was the fact that he was sad a catalyst for me to try to make people laugh? In other words, to make him laugh – seems a bit obvious, but I never was subtle.

What is obvious is that the cold, critical parent has a far more detrimental effect on the psyche of a child than one who occasionally loses it and shouts at their kids. Many of you will know what it is like to grow up with a parent who is frightening to you for whatever reason, be it drugs, alcohol, or a mental health problem. A child is totally at the mercy of the changing moods of their parents, and that can be very damaging and have a serious knock-on effect on their later life.

I talked earlier about class-based parenting. The richest people, because of their traditions, have the path of their children joylessly mapped out until they are roughly ninety years old. I remember seeing a clip of film in which Prince Charles arrived at a station to be greeted by his mum, the Queen (either he'd been at school or she'd been away): no hugs or kisses; she just walked up to him and formally shook his hand. (No wonder he started talking to plants so enthusiastically.) As a parent, it is important to look at your children and ask yourself, What sort of children are they and how do they react to you? If they hide behind the fridge every time you come into a room, it's time to re-examine what sort of parent you are.

It is the pushy middle-class parents who make the most out of what government institutions are on offer, be that health services or education services. They will make sure, because they are assertive, some might say aggressive, that they get the absolute best for their children out of education, whether their child is at a private school or a state school.

That leaves us with the working classes. That is an odd definition to use these days, because class feels such a fluid thing. But we live in a world divided between the haves and the have-nots. I suppose the working classes are the have-nots or at least the 'have-less's, people earning under a certain amount, which is not very much per year, some living slightly hand-to-mouth. These are the people who suffer the most in pushing for the best for their children. A lot of working-class families have both parents working very long hours to make ends meet, and in that case they might not have the time to spend reading *The Decline and Fall of the Roman Empire* to their children. The pushy-parent gene tends not to be present in the lives of working-class families who are struggling and there tends not to be a monetary safety net if the child fucks things up in some way.

Everyone has ambitions for their children, but depending on which part of the planet they are on, these have to be realistic. It doesn't do any good for parents to give their children absolutely everything they want, however much money they have. I have met children from every class who have been thoroughly spoiled by their parents and tend to turn into rather unpleasant adults with a whopping sense of entitlement, which now and again I have taken some satisfaction in squashing.

Things I've Learned

I became a parent pretty late in the day and have found it an enjoyable, enormous challenge (and totally crap sometimes). Here are things I've learned. I'd ignore them if I were you.

1. As a woman pushing a buggy, you become completely invisible so now is the time to try shoplifting if you are that way inclined.
2. Breastfeeding in public is worse for some people than murder.
3. If you are over forty and have very young children, they are constantly referred to as your grandchildren.
4. Total lack of sleep makes you a horrible person. I used to do a joke about getting flowers after a bad night's sleep and saying to the delivery person, 'Suppose I've got to find a fucking vase now?'
5. Don't ever tell off or criticise other people's children or the parents will get a contract out on you.
6. Trying to find out what's wrong with a five-month-old baby is just as difficult as trying to find out what is wrong with a fifteen-year-old.
7. Colic is another word to describe crying a lot.
8. When you're about to shout at your children, ask yourself, 'Is it just because I'm in a bad mood?' The answer is yes.

9. Doing your children's homework does not help them.
10. Accept most other parents are as bonkers as you but just disguise it better.
11. Any parent who tells you their eighteen-month-old can read a sign in the park needs locking up.
12. Things you think are funny about your children aren't funny to anyone else, although I did think an Easter card made at school was hilarious: 'Happy Easter and Don't Forget Jesus is Dead!'

Nagging

I prefer the phrase targeted, intelligent advice. Sometimes just for fun I used to count how many times I asked my daughters to do something before it got done (or didn't in many cases). It is good to play pants roulette – who will cave in first and pick them up to put in the wash. Let's be honest, it's pretty much going to be you every time.

I would also like to entertain you with my children's best surly responses to my entreaties, but I don't really possess a memory.

The Importance of Trust

I'm a great believer in letting children develop their own moral code and personality. Obviously start small and build. Don't begin by giving them the choice of what they eat and when they go to bed or you will have a 200 kg under-slept maniac with no teeth. Getting children to say please and thank you is hard and many parents give up after they have asked their children 5,687 times in a day. I persevered and am now inappropriately angry when a child just takes something and walks off.

As for policing what your children watch online, I think that's pointless as they know their way around a computer a squillion times better than you do. I would far rather that my children decided what to watch based on thinking and talking about it and I am hazarding a guess here – I could be wrong – that my children do not spend all their time watching porn. I'm going to ask them, so I'll tell you later what the answer is.

How to Get Over Being Embarrassed by your Parents

Just accept this isn't going to happen and things will be fine. Even the coolest famous mum/dad on the planet (insert your fave here – for me it's the Duchess of Cambridge and as I can never remember if that's Kate or Camilla, that statement is of no use whatsoever) cannot avoid their children blushing furiously and slinking off at the sound of any interaction outside the family. This gets slightly better after the teenage years but is always there to a certain extent. My children are always asking me with a pained expression not to say or do something I am intent on – and sometimes I obey them!

18

KEEPING HEALTHY

I went to my GP and asked if it was too late for me to get fit and healthy. He said it wasn't and told me do something twice a week that got me slightly out of breath. So I started smoking again.

I am obviously the last person on earth to be giving health advice to anyone and that is perhaps why I'm the best person to do it, because I know all the pitfalls and, believe me, there are plenty of people who would like me to fall into a pit.

If you look at fitness videos, health shows, weight-loss shows and all the information on the internet about dieting and getting fit, they are always presided over by some seven-stone-flicky-haired-rosy-cheeked-ball-of-irritating-energy that you just wish would go away. I think that many of us just feel envy verging on homicide when we observe this superhuman race that make it look so easy. The appearance is all – and that is why female TV celebrities are accused of cheating by having their insides scooped out, or whatever it was, to get thin enough to credibly present a fitness video. And then anyone who has the temerity to have a gastric band fitted is sneered at for their lack of having to suffer the extended punishment period a diet brings. And woe betide anyone who has a gastric band fitted and conceals it: they must be hunted down and tried as a witch, as poor Fern Britton found out.

Yes, guys, the British public wants you fat, chain-smoking pissheads out there to suffer for your health renaissance. It's not supposed to be easy for you, geddit?

That's why fat people are endlessly humiliated on weight-loss shows, placed on great big scales like swings, and to be honest I'm surprised they don't put in a creaking sound effect and the noise of cracking wood to boot. Only this way can we be beatified by the diet endurance test leading us to a magic world of acceptance.

So let's risk some advice that's not about *a diet* but about *diet*.

If you have ever wondered why you're going through life grimacing at joy and sneering at flowers and you've investigated many possibilities and not arrived at a satisfactory answer, why not . . .

Try cutting bread out of your diet and seeing how it affects your outlook.

I love toast, baguettes, rolls, naans, pizza, pitta, you name it – all of them except brioche, because bread isn't supposed to be sweet; no wonder Marie Antoinette thought it was cake. (Well all right, some amateur translator then.)

Bread makes me feel terrible physically and mentally – mainly mentally. It's the antithesis of heroin. I eat it because I love it and yet down the line lie Irritability, Negativity and Mild Aggression, three relatives of the Menopause Monster. It's an eater's version of the menopause mood, except it's less dangerous to passing males.

But that's crap, you're thinking. Obviously, because a lot of people can eat bread and not suffer any negative consequences. We thought this book was going to give us proper, subtle, helpful advice.

Some of you might not get the emotional disturbance I get, but suffer bloating. I don't bloat, as it were. I've got my own natural bloating, thanks very much for asking.

I'm also not dismissing all the other serious mood disturbers like depression or alcohol dependence. But if you could feel better merely by firing a baguette out of the window, wouldn't you try it? Grumpy and comatose – that's what bread does for me.

It took me a long time to come to this realisation, many nights on the motorway on my way home from a show in Leeds or a student gig in Loughborough, wondering why I was starting to drop off at the wheel and why I wanted to shoot all the other motorists on the M1, and then coming eventually to the conclusion that it was completely down to the very healthy diet of a stand-up: no early evening meal – too nervous – but a sandwich in the car on the way home; fatal, almost, on a couple of occasions.

I should add that this theory is not research-based but having Googled it a few times there are quite a few people who suffer and there do seem to be some very tenuous links between diet and depression, but not enough research has been done to date.

The downside of not eating bread or anything with flour in it is that the only decent substitute is crisps – okay, potatoes and we all know you have to eat a hundred-weight of them to feel full up. (Though potatoes and rice are quite nice.) Rice cakes, gluten-free pasta etc., none of these can ever hope to surpass the joy of a fresh white baguette and salty butter.

And I'm not good at cutting it out. I eat it when it doesn't matter if I fall asleep or get really moody; ask my husband, he loves those days.

According to other people, but I must admit not something I practise very efficiently, good health begins when you are extremely young, and keeping yourself in good health carries on throughout your life. Things have changed so radically from when I was a child. My parents didn't have a huge amount of money, so they fed us what was a reasonable diet for the times, but somewhat carb-heavy, hence my lifelong addiction to bread and the like. We would have porridge for breakfast, and a few bits of vegetable and fruit were shoved our way every day, so I think we did the five-a-day without even realising. They weren't heavy on sweets either, so how on earth did I put on all this weight?

It all started when I was fifteen and I was actually a normal size and I ate normally. Then I went on the pill and I put on three stone in six months, which obviously proved a very effective contraceptive. From that point on, I always assumed that once I stopped taking the pill, it would all miraculously fall off, but it never has.

So, it has been . . . I wouldn't call it a battle, because it is not that exciting, but it's been a slog trying to keep down to a reasonable weight. I think if I seriously ate everything that I really want to eat, I would probably be about fifty-five stone because, believe it or not, I do limit what I eat.

Prevention Is Better Than Cure

Let's start with preventing health problems. The message here is, don't do stuff that will cause issues for you further down the line. We all know who the big boys are in this health prevention journey.

The first is drugs. It is not a good idea to take drugs, because although they don't do chronic damage in the sense that alcohol does, drugs can be very dangerous if you don't know what you are taking. They can do extreme damage to your brain and you and there is no way of knowing that before you take them. So I would say, don't take anything to excess. I didn't always obey that edict myself, I'm afraid; I took quite a lot and survived to tell the tale, but the bald facts are that some people don't make it, and that is very sad indeed.

The same goes for alcohol. It can be acutely danger- ous if you drink a massive amount and your body can't tolerate it, but on the whole, long-term abuse damages you more over time. Lots of teenagers like to drink – there is always a shop in their local area where a very nice, helpful person will sell alcohol to under-age people – and they sit in the park and swig a bit of whatever now and again. But the kinds of people who stay hard-core with drink from those teenage years and carry it through to their fifties and sixties are the ones who are doing proper long-term damage to their livers, and who will potentially get themselves in trouble further down the line.

Obviously, it goes without saying that cigarettes are not a good idea. It is too much of a lottery. There are hale and hearty people in their nineties who have smoked sixty fags a day for their whole life since they were three, but those people are few and far between, and hoping that you will be one of them is not a very good health policy. It's a complete pain to give up and once you have, any smoke that drifts towards you in the future will try and tempt you back towards the demon fag, so it is actually much easier not to start.

Which brings me back to fatness, obesity, call it whatever you like – and whatever you call it, it sounds grim. Being fat is not healthy; it clogs bits of you up, it stops blood flowing properly through your veins and arteries, it makes your heart work a lot harder, and you could really do without it. The problem is, I do genuinely believe that there is a continuum along which fat people and thin people live, and I think thin people who eat normally are very different creatures biochemically from fat people who can't stop eating.

I remember reading an interview with Robbie Williams, who said he thought about food all the time, and some days I know how he feels. It is a modern disease that affects many of us. All right, a lot of it is to do with food being easy to buy and in front of us, but it is also a problem for people who don't live next to a supermarket or keep attractive-looking food at home. So there is something going on here. I suspect that in many years to come, they will find out the chemical that influences our appetites, and they will either turn it down or turn it up again and, lo and behold, we will all be about the same size. But that time is a very long way away, so lots of us have to try and rein things in now.

The big problem with dieting is that most fat people eat too much, so when you diet, not only do you have to drop one level to eating what normal people eat, you have to drop below that level again and eat restricted calories to lose weight. So that means you are dropping two levels down from the food that you would normally eat, and for many people that is simply too difficult, and that is why it fails. One problem is that a lot of people use eating as medicine. We have either learned through treats as a child or the comfort of chocolate and so it is a very hard habit to break.

If you look at various diets they will allow some calories in the day to 'have a treat', and this will either be two squares of chocolate or ten cashew nuts. Treat?

Hahahahahahahahahahahahahahahahahahahahahaha-hahahahahaha!

The other thing about fatness is it's so VISIBLE and it reveals to everyone you are ... Here you can insert whichever adjective best applies to your attitude towards fat people:

Greedy.
Lazy.
Depressed.
Uncontrolled.
Mad.

The fact is a moral tag is always attached to fatness and your progress through life if you're carrying extra weight will often be referred to in this way by strangers.

We've looked at some of the big don'ts, so let's look at the smaller don'ts.

Maybe don't lie in the sun and get burned all the time, don't eat too much red meat, or do stupid sports like somersaulting backwards off the top of a cliff with skis on . . . you know what I mean.

Be aware, if you live in areas that are heavily polluted, how you can best avoid those particles getting inside you; don't live in a house with loads of asbestos; and be mindful of other very dangerous materials, too – living near a nuclear power station is probably not great either, despite all the reassurances.

There are four simple things that really will help.

Eat the Right Things

We could all cut down on meat and too many carbs, eat loads of vegetables and more fruit. Clearly that is going to be hard for kids whose parents have allowed them to eat only jam sandwiches from the age of nought. But there are loads of people online who can tell you how to make your children eat healthier food, even how to hide chopped-up vegetables in cake and stuff like that when they are not watching (health by stealth), so there is no excuse these days for getting scurvy.

Know Your Family History

Some families do have a genetic disposition to certain cancers or diseases. If that is yours don't hide your head in the sand – make sure you go to regular screenings and check-ups. It's as well to be prepared and take pre-emptive action unless you want to hold your breath for thirty years.

Avoid Stress As Much As You Can

All I can say to that is, hahahahaha! No, that is not going to happen to most of us, is it, because it is unavoidable.

Exercise

Try not to get stressed about stress and remember that there is one simple thing you can do that will help enormously with everything: exercise. Now this is something everyone is really bad at these days, despite those jolly-looking government websites with green and red cartoon people bouncing up and down. Our exercise levels are pretty low because we live in a very sedentary society and most people's jobs aren't physical any more, therefore we have to replace what we are losing in physicality at work, outside in our leisure time.

Despite what many people might think, I do exercise quite a lot. I love walking. At one point when I was training for a big charity walk, I was doing five to six hours' walking a day, which I really enjoyed. But it is a bit time-consuming, so you need to find the sort of exercise that condenses that five-hour amount of energy into half an hour a day, if you possibly can.

I know we're always told that exercise is good for you, but I'm not sure you know how good. A physiotherapist I know told me that 150 minutes of moderate (i.e. breathless but still able to speak in complete sentences) exercise a week, for example, improved the relapse rate with bowel cancer by 35 per cent – yes, that's 35 per cent!!!! And she said if that had been a new drug, people would be singing about it from the rooftops, but they don't because there's no money to be made from it. Cynical? Yes, indeed.

The thing about exercise is that it's an ordeal for a lot of people, particularly if you go to the gym. The gym is for people who are already fit, not for red-faced puffing piglets like me. You go in the changing room and it's as if that film technique is running in which the background becomes fuzzy and your outline is exaggerated, pushed forward and enlarged as the healthy thin people in the room all stare at you as if you'd just walked into a remote pub on the Yorkshire moors.

But yes, exercising can be fun and the rules for that are:

Don't Do It on Your Own

Every couple of months a group of us meet up – thirtyish, a mix of adults and kids – and go for a walk in the countryside.

Build in Something Nice

We build in a meal in a pub at the end of it, so we don't have to go home to low-calorie snacks (was there ever such a depressing phrase?).

Rotate the Responsibility for Organising It

Then you don't get fed up.

Have a Laugh

Someone always falls over or hurts themselves and as long as it's not very serious there's always some good slapstick. My favourite moment of our last walk was a very steep hill at the end and a pub at the top and on arrival seeing a defibrillator attached to the wall of the pub.

Also, group exercise can be a good laugh; a lot of middle-aged portly men play footie on a Sunday morning, so why not netball, rounders or anything really in a little group in the park? Make it enjoyable; exercise doesn't have to be a solitary, sweaty, miserable slog.

For instance, some years ago I did a show for Channel 5 called *Big Splash* (no, not the diving thing) where I took part in loads of different events involving water.

- The Maldon Mud Race: a race through a muddy estuary and slowcoaches pay the penalty of sinking deeper into the mud. I had to be pulled out of the mud by a man with waders and a lasso. Not humiliating at all. Got fed up, cheated by walking along the edge to the end. Had mud ground into my face by a *Blue Peter* presenter. Yes, a fucking *Blue Peter* presenter.
- White Water Rafting: while trying to perfect the technique of getting into the raft, catapulted myself forward too quickly and landed face first in the instructor's crotch. Interesting.
- Cold Water Swimming: in Tooting Bec Lido in Feb, temperature 4 degrees. Signs everywhere saying 'Risk of Hypothermia. Only Swim One Width'. The director made me do three.
- Wild Swimming: swam in a huge lake in Cambridgeshire with Bill Bailey. One of the best days of my life.
- Driving an Amphibious Vehicle on the Road and into a River: not quite as James Bond as it sounds. Fine on the road, but like being in a shoe box in the river. Genuinely thought it was going to overturn and throw us out. It went about 0.00003 miles an hour, sorry knots.
- Holding my Breath in a Big Fish Tank: trying to beat the world record holder-of-breath. He did 17 minutes. I did 13 seconds because I started laughing.

- Sea Fishing: out in a tiny boat four miles off Lowestoft fishing for mackerel. The cameraman and I struck down by seasickness. I haven't been in a boat since.

So, as far as physical health goes, we know the basic rules, and I think if you can cling to a few of them, and do as much exercise as you can manage, that is really all that can be done without being bored shitless. As far as looking after our bodies is concerned, there's been an increasingly concerted effort by the government to ensure that we are all healthier. They have made us stop smoking, they've made us stop drinking, and now fat is the new smoking and drinking combined.

Fat-shaming is a phrase that has been dignified with an existence and it's just about abusing people who are fat. Many fat people can tell you they trudge through life dealing with outright abuse shouted out of cars or sarcastic comments from relatives who think it's all right to comment on our relationship with the scales.

The attack is severally pronged and comes from arseholes, doctors, fitness gurus. By now, nobody can possibly think fat is a great thing so all the people you see have either tried or are trying to lose weight and feel shit about themselves. So bloody leave them alone.

We are waging a constant battle against our bodies doing exactly what they want to do. This seems somewhat ridiculous to me, because we're told to give up smoking, give up drinking, be slim and get fit, which means we live a lot longer; but unfortunately, by the time we get to that very old age that we have ensured for ourselves by being fit and healthy, there won't be enough facilities available to look after us, we'll clog up the hospitals and everyone will hate the bed-blockers that we have become. So, I don't really understand the point of all that and it does make me feel like I want to smoke and drink and eat till I weigh forty stone then I can hire myself out as a bouncy castle.

19

STAYING SANE

How many therapists does it take to change a lightbulb?
Only one but the lightbulb's got to really want to change.

Roughly a fifth of people in this country suffer from depression and that is a huge number. Attitudes are changing gradually; depression isn't hidden and discussed in hushed tones in the way it was, but with any transition from ignorance to knowledge there is always a group of trailing Neanderthals who cannot or will not be carried along by the prevailing national sentiment. These people say things like 'If only they'd pull themselves together,' and that's no bloody help at all.

My dad, because of the somewhat stiff-upper-lip times he lived in, was so embarrassed about feeling the way he did that it took him forty years to seek any help. He was one of the lucky ones. The pills *did* work for him and his life was transformed. He split up with my mum when I was fourteen and I think this added to his depression.

My parents didn't exactly keep us in the loop when we were younger and we didn't have the first clue that my dad was anything but horrible and bad-tempered at times – and also prone to lash out on occasion. Not only that, but in the olden days, children, men were not really allowed to show any emotional weakness at all or they were executed. Family roles were prescribed by the society and controlled, which is why my mum got very frustrated with the house-wife part among other things and left my dad.

So it was only much later as adults that we children really became aware of what had been happening all through our teenage years. All the 'taking time off work to write', outbursts of rage and general emotional absence were just accepted. Even once he got help my dad wasn't the easiest person to discuss his mental health with. We were just relieved he was happier.

These days, we are a little more likely to deal with our mental health problems without embarrassment or shame, although it is still the educated well-off who have access to the best services through a combination of money, nous and pushiness.

The rest of society just has to get on with it and do the best they can with a creaking NHS splitting at the seams and helpful advice from the School of Hard Knocks as represented by some of the tabloids and certain ancient MPs who would say cold showers and beatings did them no harm whatsoever but that, we can tell, just by listening to them for five minutes, is simply not the case.

I believe there's a real crossover point with creativity and mental health problems. Look at people like Spike

Milligan. Plus I think it's very interesting – out-of-the-ordinary people have a lot to teach us.

As a psychiatric nurse I met people who taught me about humour, about how enormously your upbringing impacts on your adult life; I met really damaged people who were trying to put themselves together, people with drug problems, or a pattern of family stuff. It taught me about not presuming things. People tend to think of domestic violence as a working-class problem, and you realise all your presuppositions are totally wrong. It runs all through the different classes and it's about your personality, and nothing to do with your economic status.

I'm always surprised that the world is not in more of a mess than it is when you hear there's a whole raft of people who come from rough areas with terrible childhoods and it's amazing that they haven't done something criminal. People are incredible at meshing together to make a society, when a lot of them are struggling. We only know a really tiny bit about what the brain does. On a clock we're ten seconds into understanding all that we can about it.

How to Ask for Help

Generation Z and Millennials are apparently the most anxious generation. And in some ways it's easy to understand why: they are beset by bad news, constantly judged online and seemed ill-equipped to deal with the demands that society places on them. So what can be done?

Those of you who have not suffered from depression or think the sadness that overcame you when you only got a B in your physics exam counted as depression may perhaps find it hard to understand just how overwhelming depression is and just how hard it can be to seek help for it (and men are notoriously bad at this).

There are many options:

Friend: if you feel they will respect your privacy.

Teacher: don't if you feel you can't really trust them.

GP: if you like your GP and they're not aged a hundred and rather backward-looking.

Online information: there's a brilliant organisation called Young Minds who you can speak to without having to go through any 'authority' figures.

Sometimes there isn't a magical cure but admitting the problem is a good step forward, plus you feel some relief that you've done it. If you decide to visit your GP, who will have the obligatory seventeen and a half seconds to diagnose your problem and sort it, it is perhaps a good idea to go prepared with a list that allows you to remember and express all the ways depression is affecting your life. If you feel fobbed off at any point, i.e. if they write out a prescription for antidepressants almost straight away, then try and say so at the time. You have a right to decent treatment. And for depression there are several approaches.

Antidepressants

I won't blind you with science but suffice to say anti-depressants mainly try to up the level of serotonin in your body. Serotonin is what's known as a neurotransmitter and it sends messages between nerve cells. Low levels of serotonin are associated with depression. Antidepressants work well with some people and not others and different ones work better for different people so there will be a trial and error period.

Counselling

Other options range from pragmatic strategies to different types of counselling and hopefully your doctor will pick the right one for you. If at any point you feel your GP is not managing your problem very well, you can always be referred for a psychiatric outpatient's appointment.

Alcohol is not recommended because, although lots of people medicate themselves with alcohol to deal with social anxiety, it's not brilliant in the long run.

On psychotherapy, which is more long-term and involves a fairly rigid structure dictating the relationship between you and your therapist, my feeling is that it's not particularly suitable for younger people because the process can be long and drawn out and doesn't address the immediacy of a lot of teenagers' problems.

However, if you think that it's just as good having a chat with your mates to sort your depression out, you're wrong. For a start-off, therapists have trained for many years and why would they do that if one of your mates could sort you out? Second, a therapist is an objective outside force. Your friends will have a very personal perspective on you as a friend and this will get in the way.

One thing I think it's important to get clear is the burning question of how much control people have over their depression – back to the old idea of pulling yourself together. First of all this is complicated because of the issue of whether your depression is a diagnosed condition or whether it is part of what is known today as an emotionally unstable personality disorder. I'm reluctant to go into this here, because this is not a mental health manual, but suffice to say that anyone who has a personality disorder cannot separate any signs of depression from their personality, whereas someone who has depression has that on top of whatever type of person they are.

Ensuring your mental health

There are several issues here. First of all, bear in mind whether you have a family history of mental health problems and if you do, then I would put some preventative measures in place and think it is a possibility that things that have run in your family for a few generations might affect you as well.

Speak to your GP as often as you feel you need to, at any sign of something happening, like when you are feeling really low, or you have a terrible panic attack. Don't leave it and think it will go away.

Talk to someone, or look online; there are so many websites where people talk about their personal experiences that will match with yours, I'm sure.

Don't be embarrassed to seek help for mental health problems. Men generally, but young men in particular, do tend to conceal any sense of a feeling happening inside themselves, in order to keep pace with their peer group, and that concealment is what causes the stress. My father didn't seek any help for his depression until perhaps his mid-fifties, by which time he really needed a lot of it. If you catch things earlier, that can only be a good thing.

Where I worked was the nearest thing to a psychiatric A&E. Anyone who wanted to have a psychiatric assessment could literally walk in through the doors and see somebody. Mostly those we saw were people who were known to us and whose condition had deteriorated in recent weeks. They were brought in by desperate family members. Other people had never been before and were worried about things like anxiety and depression, or drugs and alcohol. Some days we would see thirty people and other days five. By its very nature the place could be chaotic, there could be abuse and violence and on occasion we would have to restrain people to stop them hurting themselves or others.

As you may have gathered this is not a formal reference book. Some of the things I've been suggesting are obvious common sense but it doesn't mean that people do them. My key bit of advice on being healthy is do more exercise.

The key thing I learned from my years as a psychiatric nurse is don't isolate yourself. If you don't have any friends and feel lonely, it is incumbent upon you, difficult as I know it is, to force yourself to make more contact with other human creatures. It is really important, because it is those people who isolate themselves for very long periods of time who can fall into a pattern of becoming depressed.

I'm not being flippant by saying 'don't isolate yourself, don't be lonely' when we know that hundreds of thousands, if not millions of people in this country live on their own and are intensely lonely. But I think that is because they could often have made the effort when they still felt reasonably okay, and they didn't. Being paranoid, or being miserable, is so much easier when you don't have other people to match your own experience against.

There are websites, and there're loads of wonderful things going on – you don't need to be on your own, there are hundreds of charities crying out for people to give a bit of their time to help.

20

GETTING ON A BIT

People always say they don't want to be shoved in an old people's home, stuck in front of the telly and being fed three times a day. Sounds bloody brilliant to me.

When you're young you want to be older and when you're old you want to be younger. This is a bit of the grass is greener syndrome coupled with the approach of the Big D, not to mention your increasing awareness of the extent of your uselessness as far as society is concerned. And on that cheery note, let's look at the positives.

The good thing about getting older is that actually you care less what people think of you and it's a relief. I think if you were very beautiful as your younger self, the physical evidence of the ageing process is so much more traumatic than if, like me, your looks have only ever been a source of negativity (particularly for me in the tabloid press). Now I couldn't care less and to some extent neither could they because they tend to ignore older women, and that suits me just fine.

Getting older isn't quite what it used to be a hundred years ago because, let's face it, people didn't really get that much older back then. Most of them were settled into their coffins before the age of seventy. Whereas these days, with improved health care, preventative medicine and so on, seventy is the new twenty. It is much easier than it used to be to disguise how old you really are, although if you have a lot of work done to your face you inhabit this weird neverland, where you look as if – I apply this equally to both sexes, because it is becoming nearly as popular for men as it is for women – they could be eighty or fifty-five. The trouble is that the older you get, the more work you need to have done, and the greater the likelihood that you will end up looking like the result of a Frankenstein experiment gone wrong.

Ageing can be a massive issue for beautiful women, who are assessed purely on their looks, in a *Love Island* kind of way, and the question of whether they have a personality or not is neither here nor there. That would really piss me off. I would far rather have heckling shouts of 'Ugly old bird!' or whatever than have people talk to me as if I was a complete moron. As someone who has never been a model (surprising news, I know), or never had a particularly gorgeous body, or indeed a gorgeous face, I have had a load of abuse over the years about the way that I look, and while I don't think I am pretty, I do think my face is all right.

*

The ageing process is something we're all aware of and without blinding you with science (as if I could), it seems to me it's all about drying up and decaying (yum, sounds lovely, doesn't it?). That's why we get wrinkly, we have crow's feet round our eyes and women who have smoked a lot look like a sewing novice has tacked round their mouth and gathered it in a bit. Hair goes grey and I find it utterly hilarious that it is fashionable to dye your hair grey if you're under thirty. Sight and hearing fail – and at least you can't see people ignoring you and hear people slagging you off. Bits that have worn out need to be replaced – like your teeth, your hips and your face.

And if there's one expression I find excruciating, which is class-ridden, misogynistic, disrespectful and pure snobbery – no, it's not the word 'chav', although I absolutely detest that as well – it's the phrase 'bingo wings'. Contained in that is the contempt of the young, wealthy male for the older, poorer woman. That is why we are constantly being told to cover up our arms because they are not attractive to look at any more given that underneath them hangs skin that people don't want to look at. Well, fuck you, I refuse to capitulate! My arms are out and proud.

Admittedly they're not on show often, but we women have had to put up with the ridiculousness of men's bollocks for ever. No pharmaceutical company has ever used them to test anti-ageing cream on – a perfect opportunity missed.

Put like this, old age sounds shit, doesn't it? And it is for many people. The more you need to be supported financially, physically and socially, the more you find yourself disappearing, because old people, unless they've acquired themselves some status like money, reputation, or celebrity, are pretty much invisible when they die. But on a more cheery note, folks! Well, is there a cheery note? If you're healthy and relatively wealthy, yes. If you're poor and in bad health, not so much so.

So what's the essential factor missing so far in what I have described? It's *attitude*.

THE CHANGE ITSELF

It's strange to think of your body as a machine with built-in obsolescence like most washing machines and microwaves today. The reproductive part of the female body is constructed to cease being reproductive around the age of fifty and yet women tend to live much longer than men. The evolutionary argument for this is these older experienced women were useful to look after the tribe's children (something that older women have been trying to escape from ever since), whereas once the men weren't up to outrunning the odd sabre-toothed tiger there wasn't much call for them.

And of course the transformation from fecund female to dried-up old hag involves the lovely bridge of the menopause with its overheating, bad-temperedness and desiccation. Sounds a delight, doesn't it?

Again, I think the menopause is slightly a matter of attitude. If you're determined to suffer, suffer you will. I managed to ignore it mostly. So you get a bit hot? I can think of worse things. As for the desiccation, help is available if you do want to carry on having sex with your husband. I sense quite a few heads shaking.

Often GPs will ask you for the date of your last period and thanks to Morrissey I can say it was on his fiftieth birthday, 22 May 2009, when I went to his birthday party in Manchester. Unforgettable.

When I was a child, ageing was a fairly uniform process, because most women over the age of fifty looked pretty much the same. Class-wise, obviously, there was a bit of a difference. If you were from the working classes and you were in your fifties, you tended to have one of those pinnies, like an overall that goes over your head, and you might have some curlers in, or you would have a perm, and as your hair went grey you would have a tint in it, mainly a blue one. Middle- and upper-class women were more likely to go for the suity-type look and a pair of K Skips, which are horribly sensible old-lady shoes that I have always hated. In those days it was a failsafe way to tell if someone felt they were getting old. They bought some K Skips and started driving a DAF. Most of you won't even know what that is (yet more proof of my stagger towards senility) but a DAF is a tiny little car that no one under the age of seventy-five is allowed to get in.

Obviously things have changed massively. Today you can have hair transplants or fillers; you can have bits taken out of your bum and stuck above your eyebrows, you can do almost anything you want. But I feel sorry for the women who believe they have to keep updating themselves in the way they might update their wardrobe. Can it really be working for them, if women are still getting the message that they are only valuable if they look attractive? If that is so, it is appalling and sad – even more so if they're getting the message that their husband won't like them any more if they look a bit saggy and baggy.

In many marriages, once you are through the twenty-five-year mark, saggy and baggy is what everyone really feels inside, and saggy and baggy it is outside for me. But it feels rather tragic that so many women feel they have got to work so hard on appearing to be younger, in order to hold on to a bloke.

There is a word in Japan that means 'a woman who looks attractive from behind and yet when she turns round, she is not attractive at all', and there is also a word for the person who invented that word, and that is 'knob-head'. As a society – and I do include the women who judge women on their looks – there is a standard to which women feel they have to aspire. It's not just a female obsession: it has infected men too – all these men getting similar surgeries, dyeing their hair, or what-have-you, in order to present themselves as a more attractive, younger model. Why they can't just sit on the beach with some egg sandwiches and read the *Daily Mail*, I do not know.

One thing that has become available to women over the last few decades is HRT, hormone replacement therapy, which gives you youthfulness on the one hand and also extends your sex life, so you feel perky and up for it. My God, who wants to feel perky and up for it? I certainly don't, I'd rather have a biscuit.

*

There is a comfortableness about marriage like an old stretchy jumper you put on every day without even thinking, and there's nothing more relaxing than putting an old stretchy jumper over an old stretchy body. The comfort of a long-term companionable partnership cannot be overestimated but there are a lot of long-standing marriages that run on the very enjoyable fuel of bickering. For adolescent humans this is what you might call 'negative bants'.

My husband and I still bicker about which side of the bed he goes on, because he doesn't like it underneath.

People always say that long-married partners can almost read each other's minds. To be honest, I've got no idea what my husband's thinking – now that waterboarding is illegal.

And, just to be annoying, research shows that being married is better for the man and worse for the woman – surprise surprise! But personally I like being married because it takes the effort out of life. You don't have to look good any more, and you don't have to bother any more. That's my motto: don't look any more and don't bother! But being in an awful marriage is so much worse than being single, so it's very dependent on who you are married to really.

There has been an attempt to somewhat glamorise old age by replacing the word 'grey' with the world 'silver', allowing us to put a more positive spin on the deterioration. So next time you step out of your house and look up at the sky, recalibrate your brain and exclaim, 'Oh, look at those silver clouds!' My motto is, 'Young or old, do exactly what you want, male or female.' So, I would suggest that if you are getting older as a woman, what you need to do is not lie down and roll over. It is to be as bloody bolshie and gobby as you can, and try not to fall into the older-women clichés. If you want to know what they are, look at Les Dawson sketches online, where he is chatting over the fence dressed up as a woman. That's how a lot of older women are seen – oop north, anyway.

But seriously, folks, there are so many older women around these days who are totally and completely impressive. My faves are:

- Mary Beard for refusing to bow down to the haters.
- Michelle Obama for being more than decorative.
- Helena Kennedy for surviving as a leading woman in the tough, public school field of the law.
- Germaine Greer for still causing trouble.
- Doreen Lawrence for unswerving commitment to positive change when bitterness could have been her main companion.
- Victoria Wood for not being Oxbridge, for not caring about looking shit for laughs, for conquering her unhappy childhood and for her exquisite material.

There is an amazing poem by Jenny Joseph, which is called, 'When I am an Old Woman, I Shall Wear Purple'. She saw getting old as the moment you could truly be yourself and do and wear anything that you want to. I want to be outrageous: I refuse to dress in pastel, nylon clothes, and fade into the background with my K Skips. There's a huge outcry about the gradual creeping upwards of the retirement age as we live longer. It's obviously because of the lack of money that the government has to pay pensions that most of us have been called upon to keep working. I have always thought that continuing to work until you drop dead is a good thing. (Think about the word itself – being described as retiring is never a compliment.) When you are working, you keep a certain amount of adrenalin pumping and you are ready for business. Once you relax and sigh, 'Aaaah, I'm free of work at last and I can have a rest,' somehow your body communicates to you, oh well, there is not a great deal to live for now. Although many people are happy in their retirement, I think a much larger number are bored shitless.

There have been some unexpected bonuses to having to work longer, which is people keeping their lives going, staying sociable, not becoming isolated and, of course, earning money if they have a slightly crap pension. Now I'm not suggesting that you keep doing something you hate till you keel over. What we all need is to do something that means something – for some it's their job but for others it could be helping people. There are charities everywhere crying out for things to be done and which would also have the bonus of introducing you to a new social circle of people, so that is what I am planning to do if I am ever forced to retire. Added to which there's also the temptation of getting reacquainted with all the things that I have been trying not to do for most of my more-grown-up life, such as smoking again, getting really drunk and heckling everyone all the time.

One area of old age that concerns me is the fact of being unable to end your life if it is intolerable. I am a supporter of the charity Dignity in Dying, which cannot seem to get the government to pass a law saying it's okay, with the requisite safety checks, to be allowed to end your life. The fear always seems to be that greedy and unscrupulous relatives will exploit this although I believe this simply will not be the case if we are vigilant.

My mum is a case in point. She's eighty-three and has a fear of losing her independence in some sort of residential facility and being at the mercy of people she does not know. I'm not implying she thinks they will do bad things, just that she won't be able to decide what she does herself. So, she has asked me if I would help her when the moment comes. I agreed, although she thought that after the six o'clock news was a little early to attempt it.

Conclusion

THE FEMALE OF THE SPECIES: MORE DEADLY THAN THE MALE?

Black widow spiders kill their mates after they've had sex with them. I know a lot of middle-aged women who'd quite like to do it before.

So when are women going to take over the world and be top dogs? And how will we know when this has finally happened? I'm sure you all want to know and I would quite like to know too. Well, it may never happen – according to the World Economic Forum it's going to take 217 years just to close the gender pay gap and probably another 200 to close the thigh gap.

I do, however, think women are making great strides forward. It's pretty interesting if you're a feminist, because the aim of feminism is equality. Why not strive to take over the whole bloody lot and be the superior gender for a bit? Come on, we've given the boys a go, it's our turn as *women* to have a crack (and I put the word crack in there because I know some men, whose partners are reading this out to them while they're watching *Top Gear*, will have a little giggle at that).

In order to decide how far we have got and how far we've got to go, let's have a look at a few areas of human behaviour, which affect the way that societies function in small ways and in big ways. This is totally subjective. Please feel free to disagree and sign a petition to put me in prison on the grounds that I am too disturbed to be in society.

Let's start with leadership, which is something that traditionally was, and probably still is to a large extent, considered to be a male domain.

If you asked a child to draw you a picture of a leader, they might present you with a man wearing a crown looking like Henry VIII, codpiece proudly on display.

This reminds me of an old lateral thinking problem.

A father and his son are involved in a road accident in which the father is killed and the son is seriously injured. The son is brought to A&E needing immediate surgery. The surgeon comes into theatre, looks at the boy and with horror exclaims, 'Oh my God, that's my son!' How do you explain this? Certainly when I was a kid, people puzzled over this for ages and eventually gave up. The simple answer is of course that the surgeon is the boy's mother. However, it was so ingrained within our psyches in those days that a surgeon couldn't possibly be a woman and I wonder how different it would be today?

This is because we tend to think of certain roles, and particularly that of a political leader, as exclusively taken by men. The reason for this is partly because we have not seen that many female political leaders, although they are rapidly increasing in number, but also I think because leadership remains something that men are more comfortable with and that they and other men guard jealously. Look at the recent experience of the Australian Prime Minister Julia Gillard, who was treated in a shockingly misogynistic way by senior right-wing politicians who, for example, put together a menu referencing her body parts and thought it was hilariously funny. Australian men not living up to the stereotype at all there.

But what are the qualities that make a good leader? Decisiveness, honesty, emotional intelligence, enthusiasm, charisma: sounds like women to me. I think that women favour a more co-operative style of management and over the past thousands of years men have built a dictatorial management structure involving shouting, bullying and ruthlessness, and nowhere is this more evident than in the newspaper industry.

There is a certain group of women who only see themselves as being decent managers if they are even harder than the worst male managers. But I think inclusivity and democracy are good qualities – no one wants to work for some dictatorial arsehole.

The will to co-operate as a manager might also be something to do with the nature of women, and I am generalising here. When I was a nurse, I was a plain old staff nurse in the twenty-four-hour emergency clinic at the Maudsley Hospital in Camberwell in the 1970s and 1980s, and I applied for a charge nurse's job and, much to my surprise, I got it. But I had huge problems with moving from being 'one of the *boys*', as it were, to being a leader. I loved mucking about, and I didn't like having to tell people off, or even tick them off if they were late for work. I didn't particularly like representing the emergency clinic in meetings, either, or occasionally being in charge of the hospital, which is what happened with senior nurses. I took a very long time to adjust to being a leader, because people become suspicious of you; they naturally don't like you or trust your motives. I read a statistic somewhere that said 40 per cent of bosses in businesses have an identifiable personality disorder. I think it is probably much more than that!

If we want more women leaders, we need to look at the whole pyramid of management, because men tend to move to the top in management and, as with leadership, that is historical in the sense that it is not that long ago (relatively speaking) that women were told to stay at home in their pinnies and bring up the family, and women are frowned upon if anything related to the family takes them away from work. The anxiety many women feel and the stress they endure balancing home and work are sometimes painful. Calling it 'juggling' is underestimating how hard it is. Besides, and I apologise to any jugglers out there, juggling is very very boring. And because men feel more comfortable, more at home in the boardroom, they are more likely to interrupt women (studies show they are three times as likely), to take their ideas as their own and to generally behave in ways that, if a woman were to do it, she'd be called all kinds of names. I also think certain facets of management, such as staying late after work a lot, or going for weekends away to do team building (or Spending a Lot of Money for No Identifiable Gain, as I like to call it) with a load of colleagues in some hotel in Cheshire, is not something really suited to women. Lots of women I know find it hard to be away from their kids in the evenings or at weekends and there is no built-in empathy in the system for parents.

In terms of intelligence as a society, who are the most intelligent: men or women? In the past, men told us that they were smarter because their brains were bigger – once again, failing to understand that size doesn't matter, it's what you do with it that counts. Scientists (also men – see a pattern emerging here?) also told us that the best measure for intelligence was IQ, and apparently men do score slightly (emphasis on *slightly*) higher in IQ tests overall. But now lots of scientists (probably some of them the female of the species) are saying that a better indicator of practical, everyday intelligence is EQ – emotional intelligence – rather than IQ. And guess what? Women score better on average at EQ. Funny that.

It has been said for many years that if you teach girls and boys together, the boys drag the girls down, and the girls drag the boys up. That is why I think exclusively girls' schools have always been very high-achieving and exclusively boys' schools tend to do a bit better than mixed schools. My daughters are at a mixed comprehensive, and it is difficult for me to judge the breakdown there in the intelligence war of the sexes, so I am not even going to hazard a guess. However, girls do have a tendency to be slightly harder working when they are studying for exams than boys and they spend longer on their homework. Girls also read more, which improves their literacy and overall school performance, and in a girls' school there's less pressure for pupils to act out in order to impress their peers. And so that is another area in which boys fall down, because they don't increase their intelligence quite as effectively as girls do.

But despite this, when it comes to the top universities, something goes wrong because top universities admit more men than women. For the first time, in 2018 Oxford University admitted more women than men and maybe this is a sign of things changing for the better.

In my experience the most difficult audiences when I used to do student gigs were Oxbridge students, who were more pissed, more abusive, more opinionated and more convinced of the rightness of their opinion. With that sense of entitlement comes a whole lot of unattractive qualities. Long gone are the days when women would go to the same lectures as men and sit the same exams, but come away with a pat on the head rather than a prestigious university degree. However things aren't all rosy in the elite institutions. Year after year at Oxford and Cambridge, men get more firsts than women. Why is this?

Some people say that it's because men take more risks – which means they also fail more often – whereas women play it safe and end up with a 2:1. Other people say it's the 'bullshit factor', because men are simply better at bullshitting (now that I can believe).

To return to emotional intelligence, I think women are definitely out ahead here, because men are, to some extent – and it must be the way the majority of them are brought up – still stifling their emotional intelligence. Somehow, in relation to their peer group, they feel that they can't be seen to be empathising, and that caring and nurturing are a bit 'girly'. But I believe it is vital that we are emotionally intelligent, and the reason why mental health has been such a stigmatised area in the past is because the male sense of self was always suppressed – a stiff upper lip and all that sort of crap.

In terms of strategy and planning, I would have to give that one to men. That is because they have more experience of it and because they are very good at that slightly dry, diagrammatic exposition of planning, and women have probably not had (or even wanted) enough involvement in that area. Women are constantly told that they aren't good at maths, so it's no surprise that fewer women study economics. But that is changing. The editor of *The Economist*, who started in the job a few years ago, is a woman, and I think that has made a big difference iconically to other women who are studying economics. I want to see more women entering the field, because economists are influential in public policymaking, from setting monetary policy to designing systems to allocate donor organs. At the moment, we're seeing the world through men's eyes, and who wants only half the story?

Let's move on to creativity, and once again I have to hand that to men. Perhaps this sounds surprising – there are lots of women writers, artists, film-makers, and we generally think of the creative, humanities subjects being more dominated by girls and women.

But the reason I think men can claim creativity is different from the other ones I have discussed, because traditionally men were the creators and it is embedded in our national consciousness that they are the ones to whom we should pay more attention and fête more. In the olden days (yeah, I'm back there again) the only women who were really allowed to create at all were middle-class women, because they had an independent income and they could sit and write *Pride and Prejudice* and the like and be able to spend the time creating with no worries. Virginia Woolf famously wrote: 'A woman must have money and a room of her own if she is to write fiction.'

Having just said that, the exception to this is *Wuthering Heights*, which was written by Emily Brontë. The Brontë sisters were not well-to-do at all. When they first published their work, they published it under male names, because they were pretty sure that if they allowed their real names to be used, no one would take them seriously. (Obviously it's really hard to hold a pen when you've got big bosoms.)

When you say 'inventor' you tend to think of a middle-aged white man with mad hair, who looks like Albert Einstein or Doc Brown from *Back to the Future*. And it's true, men have invented lots of things – but so have women. And where would we be without the algorithm, central heating, CCTV, the medical syringe, Monopoly or beer, which was invented by ancient Mesopotamian women. Cheers, my dears!

Let's talk about hard work more generally now, because personally I would give this to women. The transformation from male-dominated work to nearly equal work, and possibly in the future – fingers crossed – female-dominated work, means that although both partners might be equal, it is actually women who do the lion's share of the stuff at home. French feminists have called this the *emotional load* – I mentioned it earlier: women take on all the organisation and running of a household including all the school stuff, the school uniforms, school trips, the finances of the house, the whole lot, and that is quite something added to whatever their job may be. I'm being unfair to men here, because as Theresa May said, her husband does the 'boy's jobs', which seemed to consist entirely of putting out the recycling.

Having said that, when my kids first went to primary school at the age of five or six, which will have been roughly ten to twelve years ago, there were maybe two men in the playground picking children up from school, and now I would say that balance is nearer forty–sixty, which is a massive change in ten years.

So there you go. Does that roughly reflect how far towards gaining equality we are?

I think what women would like is a world in which they can be lazy and average and yet still be superior to men, rather than having to be 2.5 times better than their male equivalent. This has been calculated by social scientists: I haven't just made this up and if I had I wouldn't be quite so restrained – I'd be suggesting women have to be ten or even twenty times better than men.

That's really shit, isn't it, that we have to be 2.5 times better just to be equal? And the fact is that a lot of men don't like women who are more competent than they are and that is why they regress to playground name-calling and attempting to belittle women. Well, I won't be belittled. I think that's evident.

I have not been scientific, this has been totally my own subjective view, but I'm optimistic about the future and I do look forward to women dominating in all areas. Hopefully in about two years' time. Should this not happen, then we have to just keep going on until it does.

I think women will have to continue to struggle for quite a lot longer than two years but to me, the main thing is we should try to stick together as a gang and support each other even though we are such a diverse group of people with very differing views. Vaguely feminist and ferociously feminist are both fine with me as long as we're all roughly on the same page and that page isn't 3. So I think there is room for a broad spectrum of feminists with no infighting, that ranges from your dungaree-wearing, short-haired, Doc Marten-wearing feminist to your beautifully made-up lipstick feminist.

See you on the barricades for a nice cuppa!

HELP AND ADVICE

Family, children and home

Centrepoint – give homeless young people a future: 0808 800 0661, www.centrepoint.org.uk

Lucy Faithfull Foundation – preventing child sex abuse: 0808 1000 900, www.lucyfaithfull.org.uk

Missing People Helpline: 116 000, www.missingpeople.org.uk

National Association for People Abused in Childhood (NAPAC): 0808 801 0331, www.napac.org.uk

NSPCC: 0808 800 500, www.nspcc.org.uk

Shelter – advice to anyone who is homeless or anyone with housing problems: 0808 800 4444, www.shelter.org.uk

Love, sex and relationships

The Lesbian and Gay Foundation – 0845 330 30 30, www.lgf.org.uk

Barnardos: www.barnardos.org.uk

Brook Sexual Health – free and confidential sexual health and wellbeing experts: text 07717989023, www.brook.org.uk

Karma Nirvana – support for victims of honour crime and forced marriage: 0800 5999 247, www.karmanirvana.org.uk

Muslim Women's Nework (MWN): 0800 999 5786, text 07415206936, email info@mwnhelpline.co.uk, www.mwnhelpline.co.uk

National Stalking Helpline: 0808 802 0300, www.stalkinghelpline.org

Positively UK – support for anyone living with HIV: www.positivelyuk.org

Relate – The Relationship People: 0300 100 1234, www.relate.org.uk

Safeline – support for men, women and young people affected by rape and abuse: 0808 800 5005 (National Male Helpline), 0808 800 5007 (Young Peoples Helpline), www.safeline.org.uk

Stonewall: 0800 050 2020, email info@stonewall.org.uk, www.stonewall.org.uk

Drink and drugs

Alcoholics Anonymous: 0845 769 7555, www.alcoholics-anonymous.org.uk

Al-Anon – for friends and families of alcoholics: 020 7403 0888, www.al-anonuk.org.uk

Drinkaware – information about alcohol and drinking, including practical tips: www.drinkaware.co.uk

Family Lives – advice for parents concerned about teen drinking: www.familylives.org.uk

Friday/Monday – information and support for gay and bi men with drug issues: www.fridaymonday.org.uk

Narcotics Anonymous UK: 0300 999 1212, www.ukna.org

National Association for Children of Alcoholics (NACOA): 0800 358 3456, helpline@nacoa.org.uk, www.nacoa.org.uk

National Drink Helpline: 0300 123 1110

Quit – Stop Smoking Quitline: 0800 00 22 00, www.quit.org.uk

Smokefree National Helpline: 0300 123 1044, www.nhs.uk

Talk To Frank: 0300 123 6600, www.talktofrank.com

Bullying

BullyingUK: 0808 800 2222, www.bullying.co.uk

Childline: 0800 1111, www.childline.org.uk

Kidscape – preventing bullying and child sexual abuse: www.kidscape.org.uk

Teacher Support: 08000 562 561 (Wales 08000 855 088)

Your body

B-eat Eating Disorders Youthline: 0845 634 7650, www.b-eat.co.uk

Daughters of Eve – working to protect girls and young women at risk of FGM: www.dofeve.org

Epilepsy Action Helpline: 0808 800 5050, www.epilepsy.org.uk

Mermaids – support for gender variant young people: 0208 123 4819, www.mermaidsuk.org.uk

NHS Urgent Care (England Only): 111, www.nhs.uk

Sands – Stillbirth and neonatal death: 020 7436 5881, www.uk-sands.org

Young Minds Parent Helpline: 0808 802 5544, www.youngminds.org.uk

Mental wellbeing

Anxiety UK: 03444 775 774, text 07537 416 905, email support@anxietyuk.org

Campaign Against Living Miserably (CALM): 0800 58 58 58, www.thecalmzone.net

The Mix – help for young people: 0808 808 4994, www.themix.org.uk

Mind – the mental health charity: 0300 123 3393, www.mind.org.uk

No Panic – support for anyone who suffers from panic attacks, phobias, obsessive compulsive disorders: 0844 967 4848, youth helpline 0330 606 1174

Papyrus – young suicide prevention Hopeline: 0800 068 41 41, www.papyrus-uk.org

Samaritans (UK and ROI): 116 123, www.samaritans.org

SANE – emotional support for anyone affected by a mental health problem: 0300 304 7000

Self Harm: www.selfharm.co.uk

Life online

Childnet – providing online information to children and young people about smart surfing and keeping a private identity: www.childnet.com

Cybersmile – online bullying help and advice: www.cyber-smile.org

Get Safe Online – advice on protecting your privacy on social networking sites: getsafeonline.org

Internet Watch Foundation (IWF) – anonymously and confidentially report child sexual abuse images or videos on the internet: iwf.org.uk

Porn Recovery UK – information and support for anyone affected by porn or cybersex: www.pornrecovery.co.uk

Revenge Porn Helpline – support for anyone affected by sexually explicit material posted online without consent: 0345 6000 459, email help@revengepornhelpline.org.uk, revengepornhelpline.org.uk

Bereavement and grief

Child Bereavement UK – offering support to families who have suffered a child bereavement: 0800 02888 40, childbereavementuk.org

Hospice UK – hospice and palliative care services: www.hospiceuk.org

Sue Ryder – online community for families and friends suffering bereavement or terminal illness: support.sueryder.org/community

Widowed & Young (WAY) – a self-help support network for anyone widowed when young: www.widowedand young.org.uk

Work and money

Be Gamble Aware – help, support and advice on problem gambling: 0808 802 133, www.begambleaware.org/confidential-help

Money Advice Service – a government-funded advisory service for unbiased money advice, including debt: 0800 138 777, www.moneyadviceservice.org.uk

Prince's Trust – helps young people aged 13–30 develop key skills, confidence and motivation to move into work, education or training: 0800 842842, email: info@princes-trust.org.uk

The Trussell Trust – community projects tackling poverty: www.trusselltrust.org

ACKNOWLEDGEMENTS

I'd like to thank my daughters Maisie and Eliza for their invaluable input and for laughing at my use of prehistoric words and phrases; my agent and friend Vivienne, who is never anything less than supportive and truthful; my friend Betty, whose expertise in the field of mental health stopped me saying stupid things; and Georgina at John Murray, whose unwavering enthusiasm left me exhausted, but (after I'd had a lie-down) also really happy and optimistic.

From Byron, Austen and Darwin
to some of the most acclaimed and original
contemporary writing, John Murray takes pride in
bringing you powerful, prizewinning, absorbing
and provocative books that will entertain you
today and become the classics of tomorrow.

We put a lot of time and passion into what we
publish and how we publish it, and we'd like to
hear what you think.

Be part of John Murray – share your views with us at:

www.johnmurray.co.uk

 johnmurraybooks

 @johnmurrays

 johnmurraybooks